Julie Stafford's

Vegetarian Cookbook

Viking
Penguin Books Australia Ltd
487 Maroondah Highway, PO Box 257
Ringwood, Victoria 3134, Australia
Penguin Books Ltd
Harmondsworth, Middlesex, England
Viking Penguin, A Division of Penguin Books USA Inc.
375 Hudson Street, New York, New York 10014, USA
Penguin Books Canada Limited
10 Alcorn Avenue, Toronto, Ontario, Canada M4V 3B2
Penguin Books (N.Z.) Ltd
Cnr Rosedale and Airborne Roads, Albany, Auckland, New Zealand
Penguin Books (South Africa) (Pty) Ltd
5 Watkins Street, Denver Ext 4, 2094, South Africa
Penguin Books India (P) Ltd
11, Community Centre, Panchsheel Park, New Delhi 110 017, India

First published by Penguin Books Australia Ltd 2000

10 9 8 7 6 5 4 3 2 1

Design by Nikki Townsend, Penguin Design Studio
Photography by Jacqui Henshaw
Food preparations and styling by Theresa Stastny
Typeset in Berkeley Book by Midland Typesetters, Maryborough, Victoria
Printed and bound in Australia by Australian Print Group, Maryborough, Victoria

National Library of Australia
Cataloguing-in-Publication data

Stafford, Julie.
Julie Stafford's vegetarian cookbook.

Includes index.
ISBN 0 670 88665 3.

1. Cookery (Vegetables). 2. Vegetarian cookery. I. Title.

641.5636

www.penguin.com.au

Front cover photograph: **Moroccan Vegetable Casserole with Cous Cous (see page 122)**

Back cover photograph: **Fresh Vietnamese Rolls with a selection of dipping sauces (see page 78)**

April 2001

We thought this might be of some use to you! Good luck.

Love Margaret.

Let food be your medicine and medicine be your food

Hippocrates

The doctor of the future will give no medicine, he will interest his patient in the care of the human frame in diet and in the cause and prevention of disease

Thomas A. Edison

For vegetable lovers all over the world and especially for family and friends who pass by my kitchen to taste food and to share in the joy of life.

Contents

INTRODUCTION

For good health and longevity, one of the best diets to choose today is one that embraces Mother Nature's foods. It includes fresh fruits and vegetables, whole grains and cereals, nuts, seeds, legumes and pulses, and fresh garden herbs – foods grown and sold in their natural state, without pesticides, herbicides, hormones or other additives like chemical colourings and preservatives. These foods contain not only vital nutrients for survival and function, they also contain phytochemicals (*phyto* from the Greek meaning plant). These are substances that protect us against all sorts of diseases, including some forms of cancer and heart disease. They also help prevent menopause symptoms in women and generally preserve our health.

Phytochemicals occur naturally in foods like soya beans, chickpeas, lentils, vegetables, fresh garden herbs, nuts and seeds and fruits. Oranges, for example, don't just contain vitamin C, they contain over 150 other important life-supporting phytochemicals. It is the synergy of all these factors working together in the orange that makes it nutritionally valuable, not just the vitamin C.

As the new millennium begins, we move beyond using food simply to satisfy our taste buds or stimulate our visual senses. We understand the role that food plays in our quality of life and in the prevention and healing of disease. Our future health is no longer just about which foods we should avoid or cut back on, such as saturated fat, sugar and salt, while simply consuming more fresh and fibrous foods. It is about consistently building variety and balance with foods that contain not only essential factors like protein, carbohydrate and essential fats, but also those that are rich in vitamins, minerals and phytochemicals. These ingredients, found in plant, not animal, foods, will play a major role in protecting us against diseases like heart disease, cancer, diabetes, osteoporosis and auto-immune disease.

Today, Mother Nature's foods are affordable and readily available. Never before have we had such an abundant supply and variety of these foods to choose from. And never before have we been quite so ready to explore food options beyond 'flesh foods'. In the past, the emphasis on flesh foods has suggested an affluent society, but often, we now realise, at the expense of that society's health.

There is today a new consciousness about food in general. We are aware of its health benefits, but there is also on offer a much more exciting range of food ingredients from different cultures, often emphasising plant foods that produce the most wonderful flavour combinations. The cuisines of Asia, the Middle East and the Mediterranean have shown us that vegetables don't have to be bland or boring and that grains can take centre stage in place of meat. These cuisines are often mixed and matched to create unique dishes of interesting flavours.

In the future some people will continue to live to eat, others will eat to live, and those who simply love to live will do both by marrying nutritional commonsense with the art of eating Mother Nature's foods, drawing on the lessons of many cultures.

Eating only Mother Nature's foods (plant foods) is not a new phenomenon. It's commonly called a vegetarian diet. And, for whatever reason, religious, humanitarian, health, convenience or just simply because you enjoy these foods, it is a way of eating that brings enormous health benefits.

A vegetarian diet, designed using a wide variety of plant foods and eaten regularly, can provide all the protein, calcium, carbohydrates, essential fats and nutrients that you would find in a typical meat and dairy-food diet. And for those who can't always get the nutritional formula requirements to match the required taste and a sensible amount of food consumption, advanced nutritional supplementation now offers a targeted and guaranteed approach to achieving balance, without the need to add further centimetres to your waistline. The solution is not necessarily about going back to flesh foods and flesh food derivatives.

There have been times in the past eighteen years when I have chosen to remove meat from my diet, minimise dairy foods and essentially eat plant foods only, for just a few days or a few weeks at a time, for the odd month here or there and even for a whole twelve-month period. I can honestly say that during those times I always felt incredibly energetic, needed much less sleep than usual, lost a couple of unwanted kilos eating more food than I normally would have and generally felt a whole lot healthier.

In her last year at school our daughter, Cassie, like so many other girls at this age, decided she simply didn't like meat in her diet any more. She had grown tired of its taste. Her preference was for fresh fruits and vegetables, rice and pasta dishes. She introduced herself to tofu, discovered that you could make easy, exciting main meals using all sorts of grains, beans, lentils and vegetables, and turned soymilk into some sensational breakfast smoothies.

Her new way of eating not only tasted fabulous, it enabled her to discard 12 kilograms easily – a legacy of a hefty appetite (from school sports and the demands of the big VCE years). It was often easy to eat the first thing in sight (and most often the wrong thing) to satisfy those insatiable hunger pangs and teenage temptations.

Cassie's chosen career path, now that she has finished school, is to be a music and theatre performer. (The voice already makes her mother and father proud.) Her choice demands that she be lean (not anorexic) as well as physically and mentally fit. It is not a time to eat frivolously, without thought or thorough planning. She is a fine athlete in training, whose body deserves nothing but the best in nourishment. She also loves to cook, so it has been ideal for her to share some time with me in the kitchen to explore the endless possibilities of what to do with all of Mother Nature's wonderful foods for breakfast, lunch and dinner. As she steps out into the big wide world of opportunities, her mother wonders, just where did all those years go?

I am no longer seventeen and I would not describe my body as that of a fine athlete, but I do desire a quality of living and longevity that I know is within my reach – if only I feed my body the food it requires often, rather than often feed it the food it sometimes desires!

This, the ninth book in the *Taste of Life* series, acknowledges that there is life after meat and that plant foods certainly deserve a prominent place on our dinner plates. It also captures the move towards healthier eating, lighter food choices, exciting, flavoursome cultural influences in plant food preparation and a philosophy that food should preferably be fresh, seasonal, prepared with innovation and with as little fuss as possible.

It aims to encourage all of us to create more meals using foods from Mother Nature's pantry, particularly those foods rich in phytochemicals.

This book is especially for Cassie, to assist her to plan a nutritionally balanced vegetarian eating regime that provides variety, sustenance and all the necessary essential nutrients and protective agents at a time in her life when she will probably need them the most and benefit from them always.

It is also for all those vegetarians who simply need some new ideas for breakfast, lunch and dinner; and for meat lovers who would occasionally like to break out of the seven-days-a-week meat-eating mould and try something different!

And it is for Bruce and me. We haven't taken meat completely out of our eating equation, but we do love our vegies, fruits, grains, nuts and seeds. We always have, and we love the feeling of energy and vitality we get every time we choose to eat more of them. For us, the future is about travelling more lightly, and definitely with a skip in our step. These recipes are helping us do just that.

Good health!

Julie Stafford

EASY VEGETARIAN EATING

The recipes that follow have been designed to help you build a healthier diet by using more plant foods and less meat and fewer dairy products in your daily regime. The recipes are not intended to fit a strictly vegan (vegetables and plant foods only), lacto-vegetarian (plant foods with milk and milk products) or ova-vegetarian (plant foods and eggs) diet, but you will find recipes suitable for all three of these.

While eliminating meat from all the recipes, the *Vegetarian Cookbook* also aims to minimise the use of animal products in general: foods such as eggs, cheese, milk and other dairy items. When these foods are included in a recipe, low-fat options or suitable substitutes are provided.

THE FACTS ON FATS AND IRON

Today, when food options are almost too diverse to think about and the statistics for obesity, heart disease, cancer and diabetes are on the rise, resulting in poor quality of life and early deaths, be aware that the number one risk factor associated with all these diseases is a diet of excessive saturated fats and lack of exercise.

Saturated fat is essentially animal fat (from animal foods and food products). Plant foods are completely free of saturated fat. They contain essential nutrients for survival and function, valuable phytochemicals and are loaded with essential dietary fibre. Some even contain essential fats of a polyunsaturated and mono-unsaturated nature that actually fight disease and improve the quality of our daily health.

Fats in plant foods and meat and dairy foods are in fact very different. At body temperature (37°C) plant oils are liquid, whereas animal fats at the same temperature are stiff and solid. Plant oils do not stick to artery walls, whereas hard animal fats do. Plant oils are mainly polyunsaturated and some are mono-unsaturated. They tend to increase the HDL (high-density lipoprotein, or good cholesterol), which helps prevent heart disease. They are high in linolenic acids, which stimulate prostaglandins 1 and 3, and these decrease inflammation in the body. On the other hand, animal fats are saturated. They tend to raise the LDL (low-density lipoprotein or bad cholesterol) and lower the HDL, which is the biggest risk factor for heart disease. They are also high in arachidonic acid, which stimulates prostaglandin 2, and this triggers inflammation in the body. Saturated fats make you fat. They serve essentially only as a source of kilojoules, whereas polyunsaturated and mono-unsaturated fats provide the body with essential fatty acids that help it perform many biological functions.

Iron, vital for growth, repair and energy, can be found in many foods other than meat. Although red meat is possibly the most recognised source of iron, closely followed by chicken and fish, iron can be found in lots of different plant foods: foods such as leafy green vegetables, nuts and seeds (especially pumpkin seeds and sesame seeds), wheatgerm, oatmeal, bran, soya beans, fresh herbs and even herbal teas.

The body absorbs iron more readily when the food containing iron is combined with a food containing vitamin C: for example, a glass of fresh orange juice with a bowl of oatmeal porridge for breakfast, or a bean dish with a salad containing red capsicums. For this very reason, in many of the recipes in this book you will find suggestions for teaming the meal with a glass of fresh juice. Delicious recipes for fresh fruit and vegetable juices can be found in my juicing book, *Julie Stafford's Juicing for Health*.

GLOSSARY OF VEGETARIAN INGREDIENTS

Agar Powder is a seaweed setting agent, similar to gelatine (an animal-derivative product). It is high in protein and calcium and easy to digest. One teaspoon of agar powder sets approximately one cup of liquid. You will need to boil the agar in water for a few minutes to dissolve it.

Apple Juice Concentrate is a sugar substitute. This syrup is used in all the *Taste of Life* cookbooks to provide sweetness in recipes, but has much fewer kilojoules than refined sugar or honey. It is actually apple juice boiled down to make a honey-like-consistency syrup. It can be reconstituted to an apple juice drink by simply adding a little to a glass of water. You'll find it at health food shops and supermarkets. Honey or maple syrup can be substituted for apple juice concentrate (remembering that these both have more kilojoules).

Cereals and Grains

Cereals and grains are important ingredients in a vegetarian diet. The most commonly used are wheat (mainly milled to make a flour, used for baking breads, cakes, muffins, pastry and pasta); buckwheat; rice; millet; corn (ground to a fine or coarse cornmeal); rolled oats; barley and rye. They are an excellent source of protein, all low in fat and rich in carbohydrates (vital for energy), B-group vitamins and minerals (especially iron and phosphorus), and provide a high component of essential fibre, especially when eaten in their whole unprocessed state.

Barley has a unique flavour and chewy texture. The whole grain is used in soups and also makes a delicious health drink known as Barley Water or Barley Broth (see the Barley Water recipe in the *Taste of Life*). Cold cooked barley can be substituted in recipes that call for cold cooked rice. It is also available in barley flakes, which are commonly used for porridge, in muesli and in baking.

Buckwheat, commonly thought of as a cereal, is actually a grass. It is the seeds of the grass that are used in cooking. It has a rather nutty texture and can be used as a rice substitute to accompany other foods, as an ingredient in vegie burgers, stuffed vegetables or cabbage-roll stuffing. The seeds are ground to make a flour used for baking.

Cornmeal (also called polenta) can be finely or coarsely ground. Yellow in colour, it brings a unique appearance, corn taste and mealy texture to breads, muffins, pancakes and polenta, and can be baked or grilled.

Cous Cous is actually small semolina pellets, made by rubbing semolina grains into white flour that is then cooked and dried. It is often referred to as the fast grain because it needs only to be soaked briefly before eating, rather than cooked like most other grains. It makes delicious salads or can be used as a base for vegetable dishes.

Cracked Wheat/Bulghur Wheat is best known for its use in tabbouleh salad. The whole wheat is steamed until nearly cooked, then dried and crushed. It needs to be soaked before using in recipes.

Millet is used extensively in South-East Asia and is cooked and used in recipes in the same way as rice.

Oats (rolled) are an excellent source of protein, thiamine, niacin and iron. High in fibre and carbohydrate energy, they are traditionally used to make a nourishing porridge or as an ingredient in muesli and are an excellent ingredient for baking.

Rice includes **brown rice**, which has three times more fibre than **white rice.** It comes in short and long grains, takes longer to cook than white rice and, where white rice has a rather bland taste, has a distinctively nutty flavour. **Basmati** and **Italian** rice are both long-grained and traditionally served to accompany Asian-style recipes and curries. Short-grained **arborio** rice is used for risotto. It releases starch during the cooking process, which makes it stick together. If using white rice (brown rice without the bran covering), add lots of high-fibre vegetables and serve with high-fibre grain breads. Like cold cooked pasta, cold cooked rice keeps well refrigerated. Use it for hot or cold rice meals. **Puffed, par-boiled brown rice** is ideal to use in homemade muesli and baking.

Rice Flakes are made by steam-cooking brown rice, then rolling the grains flat and drying them. The flakes contain all the nutrients of the original grain and are ideal in homemade muesli and rice porridge. They also make delicious creamed rice puddings.

Rye grain is milled to make rye flour, for bread baking. It is recognised by its darker colour and strong smell, some say of whisky in the making. It is also available in rye flakes, which are used in porridge (best mixed with rolled oats) or can be added to vegie burgers or used to thicken vegetable casseroles and soups.

Semolina is the milled inner endosperm (see Unbleached White Flour, page 11) of wheat. Yellow semolina is made from soft durum wheat and white is made from hard wheat. It makes a soft, delicious porridge and tasty pasta products.

Triticale (flakes) is a relatively new grain produced by crossing wheat and rye. It combines the high lysine content of rye with the overall high protein content of wheat. Like most grains that are not heavily processed, triticale is low in fat and a good source of protein and dietary fibre, and its nutty, slightly rye flavour makes it an ideal grain to use in homemade muesli and porridge, and in baking.

Dairy Foods

Dairy foods come from animals and are not acceptable in a strict vegan diet (plant foods only). They can also contain lots of saturated fat. However, because dairy products combine so well with plant foods, I have included small amounts of just some of the low-fat dairy options that are now so widely available:

low-fat ricotta cheese, low-fat feta, reduced-fat mozzarella, parmesan cheese, low-fat yoghurt and light frûche. For a strict vegan diet or if you suffer from cow's milk allergies, you can always substitute tofu for ricotta cheese; soymilk, goat's milk or sheep's milk yoghurts for yoghurt and frûche; and soymilk, goat's milk, almond milk (see page 144) and oat milk for cow's milk or buttermilk.

Cheese is most often made from cow's milk with the substance rennet (taken from a calf's gut) added to hasten the cheese-making process. You can buy rennet-free cheeses that use vegetable enzymes instead, but because cheese is basically made from milk it is not strictly a vegetarian food. Soy cheese is now available and can be used in all recipes that commonly use cow's milk cheese. It can be grated and sprinkled over recipes for extra flavour or it melts quite well on top of vegetable lasagnes and in a white cheese sauce. However, the taste is quite different to mozzarella or parmesan cheese. If you want to include milk cheese in your vegetarian diet (like mozzarella or parmesan), use it minimally. Use it to lift the flavour of a recipe rather than overpower it, and cut back on the amount you would normally use. You can combine grated cheese with breadcrumbs or finely chopped herbs to make it go further. Low-fat hard cheeses (best used in cooking) should have a fat content of less than 10 g per 100 g serve. Cheeses with a fat content over 5 g per 100 g serve should be used less often and only in moderation.

Cottage Cheese is a white creamy cheese with small curds. It has a light acidic flavour, though still fairly bland. It contains a maximum of about 0.4 per cent fat. It is suitable for savoury or sweet recipes. It is an excellent source of protein, B-group vitamins, calcium and phosphorus.

Feta Cheese (low-fat) is an uncooked white cheese with a distinctive salty taste from being pickled in a brine solution. It is typically used in Greek-style recipes.

Frûche (vanilla, low-fat) is a yoghurt-like food of firm consistency, with added gelatine and rennet.

Mozzarella Cheese (reduced-fat) is a soft cheese but firm enough to grate, most commonly used on top of pizzas and lasagne.

Soy Cheese is a soft white cheese made from soymilk. Its fat content is dependent on the fat content of the soymilk used to make the cheese.

Ricotta Cheese (low-fat) is a soft but firm, creamy white cheese made from the curd rather than the liquid cow's milk. It has a bland, slightly nutty flavour and is a mass of fine, small curd particles (much finer than cottage cheese). It is ideal to use in sweet or savoury recipes. Like most dairy foods, it is an excellent source of protein, B-group vitamins, calcium and phosphorus.

Yoghurt (low-fat) is a cultured milk product. Specific bacteria are added to warm, fresh, low-fat milk (cow's, goat's or sheep's milk is suitable) to develop a tangy-flavoured, custard-like yoghurt. It is more nutritious than milk because an extra 4 per cent of non-fat milk powder is added to enhance the texture. Yoghurt contains lactobacillus acidophilus, a healthy bacteria that is thought to help restore the balance of healthy organisms in the gut. During the yoghurt-making process, fat and protein in the yoghurt are broken down, turning lactose into lactic acid, which makes it easily digestible. Look for varieties that have a fat content of approximately 0.1 per cent fat. Yoghurt is an excellent source of protein, vitamins A and B, calcium and phosphorus.

Dried Fruits like sultanas, raisins, currants, bananas, nectarines, dates, figs, apricots, peaches, pears and apples are all rich in dietary fibre, vitamins and minerals. They are also high in fruit sugars. They make great snacks and are equally good in porridge and muesli and also for baking in cakes, muffins and breads. Buy sun-dried varieties with no additives or oil. Store in sealed jars.

Eggs are used in a more liberal or ova-vegetarian diet. They are an excellent alternative to meat in a vegetarian diet, but should not be used excessively because the egg yolk is high in saturated fats. They are rich in protein, iron, phosphorus and vitamins A, B12 and D. In most recipes, two egg whites replace one whole egg, rendering these recipes fat-free. Limit yourself to one whole egg per day and use free-range eggs for a bright yellow yolk and a thicker white.

Essences are concentrated flavourings of particular foods. Add just a few drops to a recipe to give it the distinctive flavour of the essence you are using. Some favourites include vanilla, orange, lemon and almond. They are a great addition to smoothies.

Flours

Different flours have different tastes, textures and cooking times. For the best results in baking always aerate the flour by sifting it before incorporating other ingredients. There is a wide variety of flours to choose from, including unbleached, wholemeal, soy, rice, potato and rye. All have their own unique flavours and they often combine well together. All flour should be stored in a sealed container and kept at a constant temperature.

Cornflour is a fine white flour made from corn, wheat or a combination of both. It is mixed with cold water to make a paste and used as a thickening agent. Always mix with cold liquid before adding to a hot liquid.

Potato Flour is mostly used as a thickening agent due to its high starch content. It is gluten-free and ideal to mix with other gluten-free flours to make gluten-free recipes. You will need to add a leavening agent such as baking powder.

Rice Flour is gluten-free and is milled from white or brown rice grains. It is rich in starch and fibre and gives baked goods a gritty texture. Rice flour combines well with soy flour, cornmeal or a combination of these to make a gluten-free dry mixture suitable for baking cakes, muffins or bread. You will need to add a leavening agent such as baking powder.

Rye Flour is recognisable in recipes because of its distinctive flavour and dark colour. It is most often used for bread making.

Soy Flour is processed from soya beans, which contain all eight of the essential amino acids. It adds protein, iron, thiamine, niacin, calcium, zinc and a moderate amount of fibre to your recipes. Soy flour is often combined with other flours like rice flour, potato flour and wheat flour in baking because alone, its flavour can be a little overpowering and it cooks a lot faster, rendering a very dark, almost overcooked appearance. You will need to add a leavening agent such as baking powder.

Unbleached White Flour (plain and self-raising) has the wheatgerm and bran removed by a process of continuous sifting. The endosperm (the main starchy part of the wheat grain) is ground to a very fine powder. White flour contains more gluten (the protein of the wheat) than wholemeal flour. Unlike ordinary flours, bleaches and chemicals are not added to this flour. It has little, if any, fibre.

Unbleached Wholemeal Flour (plain and self-raising) is high in fibre and contains plenty of wheatgerm and bran. It also contains more minerals and vitamins than white flour. It has a nutty taste and a mealy texture. Because of its high-fibre content it absorbs more liquid than white flour. Like unbleached white flour, this flour does not go through a bleaching process.

Fruits

Choose from a wide variety of fruits, preferably organically grown, and eat at least 2–3 or more servings every day: apples, apricots, avocado, bananas, berries (blackberries, blueberries, strawberries, gooseberries, loganberries, mulberries, raspberries), canteloupe, cherries, cumquats, custard apples, dates, figs, grapes, grapefruit, honeydew melon, kiwi fruit, lemons, limes, loquats, lychees, mandarins, mangoes, nectarines, olives, oranges, passionfruit, pawpaw, peaches, pears, pineapple, plums, quince, rhubarb, tangerines, tomatoes and watermelon.

Canned Fruits without added sugar are a good nutritional alternative to fresh fruit when fresh fruit is not available or out of season. Try to eat only fruits in season.

Herbs

Herbs not only add that burst of exciting flavour to any meal, they are a rich source of micro-nutrients that add another dimension of vitality to food. To enjoy the best taste and health properties, herbs should be as fresh as possible. Try growing some at home. Use both the leaves and stems, chopped up and scattered over a meal just before serving. I have listed some of the more popular herbs that I rely on in my cooking, but there are many others, so go exploring! The amount used in each recipe is merely a guideline and will vary according to your individual taste. Fresh herbs can be replaced with dried herbs (about 1 teaspoon of dried herbs is equivalent to 1 tablespoon of chopped fresh herbs) but the flavour is quite different. I like to keep dried herbs for recipes that require baking.

Basil belongs to the mint family. Its smell is aromatic with a sweet, licorice-like flavour. The foliage is either green or purple and it is the perfect complement to tomatoes, grilled vegetables, pasta sauces and salad greens. Chopped, it adds a delicious flavour to a vinaigrette, or by blending some fresh leaves with yoghurt and pine nuts you can make a fabulous creamy (cheese-free) pesto-style mayonnaise.

Bay Leaves have a delicious sweet flavour. Add them to vegetable soup, white sauce and pasta sauces, but do remember to remove them before serving the dish.

Chives belong to the onion family but the taste is very mild. The fine, green grass-like foliage adds a subtle onion flavour and an interesting texture when chopped and added to baked potatoes, bean, rice and vegetable dishes. It is also a popular salad and salad dressing garnish.

Coriander has delicate, wispy, pale green foliage that adds a slightly oriental, peppery flavour to recipes. A little goes a long way and you'll mostly find it used in Thai cooking.

Dill is a pungent, slightly sweet-tasting herb. Its very fine feathery foliage has a slightly aniseed taste that is ideal for flavouring potato salads and other vegetable recipes.

Marjoram is very similar to oregano, though more delicate in flavour.

Mint is mostly recognised for its refreshing, tangy taste. It adds a distinctive flavour to a vinaigrette and is excellent used in salads of tomato, onion and orange or cucumber, or you can add a few leaves to a salad of greens and especially to fruit salads. (See *Julie Stafford's Salads*.) Combine it with basil and add to vegie burgers for an Asian flavour. This is a herb best grown in a pot to contain its healthy root system to just one spot!

Oregano is an aromatic and highly flavoured herb. It features strongly in Italian cooking.

Parsley, with its rich green colour and mild, yet distinctive flavour, can be added to practically any recipe. It is extremely compatible with all other herbs.

Rosemary has very fine, spiky leaves. The taste, like basil, is strong and very aromatic. You need only a small amount. I like to add it to oven-baked or chargrilled vegetables (see pages 144–6) and use it in sauces for pasta and beans. It is also a good herb for flavouring vinegars, which can be used instead of traditional dressings to flavour a salad. Simply pour warm vinegar over some sprigs of rosemary placed in a bottle. Seal and store the herb vinegar for at least one week before using.

Thyme foliage and the flower from the shrub can both be used to flavour vegetables. I particularly like thyme with roasted vegetables, and in soups and salads that use tomatoes as a base.

Honey Although I like to use apple juice concentrate (because it has less kilojoules than sugar) in recipes that would normally call for white, brown or raw sugar, honey, maple syrup or golden syrup, there are some recipes that rely on the unique flavour of honey. Buy organic honey if you can find it. The flavour is sensational.

Juices Freshly squeezed fruit juices or fruit- and vegetable extracted juices are definitely the best. Drink them fresh any time during the day. (See *Julie Stafford's Juicing for Health*). Try freshly squeezed lemon, lime or orange juice with just a little balsamic vinegar over your salad for a delicious fat-free salad dressing.

Nori Sheets are dried sheets of seaweed used in traditional Japanese recipes like nori rolls. They are low in fat and a rich source of the minerals zinc, manganese, nickel, molybdenum, selenium, copper, cobalt and chromium.

Nuts add nourishment in the form of calcium, iron, magnesium, phosphorus and vitamin E. They are full of flavour and dietary fibre and add an interesting crunchy texture to any recipe. They are a high-energy food containing about 80 per cent mono-unsaturated fat (like the fats in olive oil). They can be added whole or chopped in their raw sweet state, or dry roasted (see page 27) for a concentrated flavour. Use only fresh nuts; preferably buy them in their shells, and break them open with your fingers as you need them – this releases more flavour from the natural oils. Store them in a dark, cool, dry place and keep for no longer than about six weeks. Because of the high-fat nature of nuts, they can become rancid and harmful to health. Include nuts such as almonds, brazil nuts, cashews, hazel nuts, macadamia nuts, peanuts, pecans, pine nuts, pistachio nuts and walnuts in your diet.

Oils

A plant-food diet should include some vegetable, nut and seed oils. They provide essential fatty acids (EFAs) necessary *for building cell structure. The body cannot manufacture these essential fatty acids, which are vital for good health. Unlike animal fat (saturated fat), which provides kilojoules with few health benefits and harmful cholesterol, vegetable fat (unsaturated fat of a polyunsaturated or mono-unsaturated nature) provides necessary nutrients and health-protecting factors without harmful cholesterol. There are two types of essential fatty acids provided by this food group. They are Omega 6 EFAs, found in sesame oil, safflower oil, sunflower oil and corn oil, and Omega 3 EFAs, found in linseed oil, cod liver oil, canola oil, almond oil, macadamia oil, olive oil and walnut oil. These oils provide more than twice as much energy as carbohydrate and protein foods, so you only need small amounts. If you are cooking with oil, keep the temperature low so you do not burn the EFAs. Use oils that are first pressed (virgin), often obtained by hand pressing, and oils that are stored in dark bottles. Always taste oil before you use it. It should be good enough to drink and its unique flavour obvious. If it looks cloudy or tastes bitter, discard it, as it is most probably rancid. I keep a good olive oil at hand for all basic cooking, occasionally using sesame seed oil in Asian cooking for its specific flavour, and grapeseed oil for baking. Other oils you might like to try for their very specific and unique flavours and health properties include safflower, peanut, hazelnut, mustard, almond, macadamia, corn, pecan, sunflower, flaxseed and walnut, or a blend of any of these.*

Carotino Oil is a blend of oils from vegetables rich in carotenes (vitamin A). It is bright orange in colour and is ideal for all vegetarian recipes that require oil in the cooking process.

Grapeseed Oil is a light, bland oil that will not overpower other food flavours and is ideal for cake, muffin, bread and pastry recipes.

Olive Oil is a staple ingredient of the Mediterranean diet, obtained by pressing the ripe pulp of the olives after picking. Its rich yellow to green colour is secondary to its fruity, flavoursome qualities. It is interesting to note that people living in the Mediterranean regions, who use olive oil in large quantities, have a low incidence of heart and inflammatory diseases. (Perhaps it's the oil. Perhaps it's the garlic, the tomatoes or the red wine, or perhaps it's a combination of all three!)

Sesame Seed Oil is used for its strong nutty flavour and combines well with fresh ginger, garlic, chilli and honey, especially in Asian-style recipes. You need only a little.

Olives Surprisingly, these small fruits are high in fat, though it is mostly mono-unsaturated fat. They also contain a lot of salt. It is their strong, sharp, salty taste (achieved by pickling) for which they are prized. Use a small amount to flavour a recipe or purée them to make a delicious paste (often called a tapenade) that brings a more concentrated olive flavour to many recipes such as pizzas, pasta sauces, pita lunch wraps and soups.

Pasta and Noodles While fresh pasta is generally preferred, both for flavour and for speed of cooking, the dried product made from flour (white or wholemeal) and water, which includes **spaghetti, fettucine, linguine, tagliatelle, farfalle, rigatoni, penne, cannelloni, lasagne sheets** and **macaroni**, is a very valuable store-cupboard ingredient. Both need to be cooked in lots of rapidly boiling water. Pasta is ready when it is soft and *al dente* (slightly firm, with a little bite left in it). Drain pasta and serve immediately with your favourite sauces or, if a recipe requires cold cooked pasta, drain pasta and run it under cold water; drain well before using. Keep a good supply of different types and shapes of dried pasta at hand. **Soyaroni** spiral pasta made from soy flour is also available and is delicious served with your favourite pasta sauce or added to soups to make a 'meal soup'. All cooked pasta makes an excellent base to which you can add a variety of cooked vegetables and sauces, just as all cold cooked pasta keeps well in the refrigerator and can be turned into cold pasta salads or reheated by placing it in a bowl, pouring boiling water over it and letting it stand for a few minutes. Drain well and serve. Oriental noodles are delicious also. Look for **hokkien noodles**, **shanghai noodles** and **soba noodles** in the refrigerated section at supermarkets. There are also different types of **rice noodles**, both fresh and dried, that take just minutes to prepare and are delicious in soups or vegetable stirfry meals.

Pulses and Lentils (dried beans, peas and lentils)

This group includes foods such as black beans, borlotti beans, butter beans, cannellini beans, chickpeas, haricot beans, kidney beans, lentils, lima beans, mung beans (most often sprouted), peas and soya beans. These foods, a popular staple in the Middle East and India and now becoming more popular in the West, are often considered the core of a vegetarian diet and are ideal, relatively cheap, low-fat foods that are high in vegetable protein (especially soya beans) and rich in amino acids. Recently, scientists have discovered that these foods contain substances called phyto-estrogens. Populations that have high levels of these foods in their diet do not experience symptoms or diseases associated with low levels of estrogen in the body.

By combining pulses with cereals you create a more complete protein similar to what you would find in meat. Pulses are an excellent source of iron, zinc and calcium but they are best combined with other foods containing vitamin C for maximum iron absorption. They are high in soluble fibre (excellent for cholesterol control) and high in starches that are digested and absorbed slowly, resulting in a slow release of glucose into the blood (ideal for controlling blood-sugar levels in people with diabetes). It is necessary to wash these foods thoroughly before cooking and some are best soaked overnight to make them less 'gassy'. Peas and beans generally absorb about double their weight in water. One cup of dried peas or beans soaked should yield approximately 2–2½ cups of cooked beans. It is also a good idea to cook peas and beans in their soaking liquid so you don't lose valuable nutrients down the sink.

Canned Pulses You'll find many varieties of cooked pulses in cans on the supermarket shelf. All you need do is rinse off the liquid they come packed in and you are ready to create a meal in just minutes. They are an excellent choice of fast food and highly nutritious.

Sprouts Most beans, peas and lentils can be sprouted. They take between 5–10 days. Once sprouted they are a highly nutritional food, rich in nearly all vitamins (especially high in vitamin C) and minerals. They are a good source of protein and dietary fibre and you can add them to just about any meal.

Tofu is a bland-tasting unfermented soya bean curd. It's made by adding a natural coagulant such as lemon juice to soymilk. Curds are created, the excess milk is drained off, and the curds are pressed into blocks to further remove all liquid. It is an excellent source of protein, rich in natural phyto-estrogens and calcium and is both low in fat and cholesterol free. It is available in a firm form, which can be grilled and added to stirfrys and noodle dishes or wrapped in pita breads and rice wrappers to make fast nutritious meals. A soft silken form is also available. It can be used in cake and muffin making, dips and dressings, and makes a delicious low-fat cream whip added to soup for a creamy texture.

Sauces

Hoi Sin Sauce is a thick, sweet sauce made from fermented soya beans. A little goes a long way in Asian-style or stirfry dishes.

Fish Sauce Made from fermenting anchovies, this sauce is traditionally used to flavour Thai and Vietnamese recipes. Choose low-salt varieties. You can use low-salt soy sauce in its place. Although not strictly a vegetarian ingredient, you only need to add such a small amount to a recipe for the desired effect, and I particularly like its taste in a couple of favourite vegetarian meals, especially Caesar Salad (see page 70).

Pesto traditionally combines fresh basil, pine nuts, parmesan cheese, garlic and olive oil. It is commercially available or you can make it yourself. Without the cheese, its flavour is still sensational and of course it is much lower in fat (see page 152).

Soy Sauce (low-salt) is an almost black, thin sauce made from fermented soya beans that adds a sharp, salty flavour to recipes.

Sweet Chilli Sauce is a must-have condiment if you like chillies. There are different varieties available, so choose one that is low in salt and sugar. You only need the tiniest amount to enjoy its delicious taste, so treat yourself.

Seeds

Sesame seeds, pumpkin seeds and **sunflower seeds** are a vegetarian pantry essential. Their nutritional make-up is similar to that of nuts. They also contain valuable phytochemicals. Nibble on them as a snack, scatter them over your breakfast cereal or main meal to add another nutritional dimension or grind a mixture of seeds and nuts to a butter consistency and use as an alternative butter spread.

Soymilk is a milk made from soya beans. It has similar nutritional properties to cow's milk without the lactose, animal fats and cholesterol. It has a nutty flavour and is used in much the same way you would use cow's milk. Low-fat and fat-free varieties are available.

Spices and Condiments

The inclusion of just a little spice or just a little of the right condiment in a recipe can dramatically transform a meal.

Allspice is a strong-flavoured spice with an aroma similar to a combination of cinnamon, cloves and nutmeg.

Capers are small unopened flower buds of the caper bush. They are pickled, usually in a white vinegar. Add them to a vinaigrette for a strong, aromatic flavour or add a few to a cooked vegetable dish, salad or coleslaw.

Carob Powder Carob comes from the long pods of the carob tree. It has no significant nutritional value, but its flavour is similar to cocoa and chocolate. As it is perhaps a little darker and richer than cocoa or chocolate, use smaller quantities of carob in recipes. Unlike cocoa and chocolate, it is free of caffeine, oxalic acid and theobromine (a chemical known to cause headaches).

Cayenne is a ground spice of the chilli pepper family.

Chilli Powder is a hot, spicy powder made from the dried seeds of chilli. Depending on your taste, add as little or as much as you like to a recipe.

Chillies (fresh) The red ones are generally hotter than the green ones. The smaller the chilli, the hotter the taste! I mostly use the red ones, as you only need a little to get the best taste. Beware of the seeds as this is where the majority of heat lies. Remove the seeds before dicing.

Chinese Five Spice is a pungent spice made up of cinnamon, cloves, fennel, star anise and Sichuan peppers.

Cinnamon is a popular and common spice that comes from the bark of a tree native to Sri Lanka. It is available whole or ground and in rolled-up quill or stick form.

Cloves are a warm aromatic spice that are often used to flavour cooked fruit recipes and puddings.

Coconut Milk Canned coconut milk is thinner in consistency and lower in fat than coconut cream. It can be further diluted with water or skim milk. To make your own coconut milk, blend ½ cup low-fat milk or low-fat soymilk with 1 tablespoon shredded coconut and strain.

Coriander Seeds are small dried seeds from the coriander plant that have been roasted.

Cumin is a warm aromatic spice often used in curry-style recipes.

Curry Paste Of the prepared curry pastes available I particularly like a hot vindaloo variety and a milder red curry paste (in both cases a little makes a big impact). Green curry paste, made from green chillies and spices, is very mild. The flavour of curry paste is much more intense than curry powder. For every tablespoon of curry powder, use only about a teaspoon of curry paste.

Curry Powder There are several blends available, mostly comprised of varying amounts of the following ground herbs and spices: coriander, turmeric, chilli, cumin, fennel, fenugreek, mustard, ginger, cinnamon, nutmeg and cloves. You can use a commercial mix or make up your own.

Garlic A peeled garlic clove added to a recipe gives a very subtle garlic flavour. Chopped garlic, on the other hand, imparts a slightly stronger flavour while crushed garlic cloves offer the most intense flavour of all. One large, peeled garlic clove is equivalent to ½ teaspoon crushed garlic.

Ginger You'll find these interesting-looking knobbly roots at the supermarket or greengrocer. Look for young ones with taut, thin skin (they are less fibrous with more juice). Remove the skin and finely dice or place small pieces in a garlic press. Ginger is prized for its sweet yet slightly spicy flavour.

Ginger (pickled) At the very best food stores you'll find a container of thin shavings of ginger that have been pickled in a solution of sugar and vinegar. The flavour can only be described as sensational. The smallest amount complements everything you might add it to like stirfries or lunch wraps.

Ginger (ground) is mildly spicy and warm. This spice is often teamed with other spices like garam masala, garlic powder, cumin powder and cardamom in curry-style recipes.

Kaffir Lime Leaves are from the kaffir lime tree and are used chopped or crushed in typical Asian-style recipes. You can substitute leaves from ordinary lime or lemon trees.

Lemon Grass is a lemon-scented grass used in Asian cooking. It is the tender root of the grass that is most prized. Chop it finely and add to recipes.

Mayonnaise Choose low-fat, cholesterol-free commercial mayonnaise. My preferred choice is a cholesterol and egg-free mayonnaise made by Melrose Health Supplies.

Mirin is a sweet white wine used in cooking. You can substitute any white wine.

Miso is a fermented soy paste used as a traditional Asian flavouring. It makes an ideal soup stock (see page 156) and can also be used to flavour stirfry vegetable and noodle dishes. I have used the dark brown miso in recipes calling for miso.

Mustard Dijon is a smooth, sharp but not too hot-tasting, creamy mustard paste. **Dry** is a finely ground powder of mustard seeds. **English** is a smooth, very hot mustard paste. **Grainy** features black and brown mustard seeds in a creamy mustard paste with a strong, pungent taste. Flavours vary depending on the quantity and quality of vinegar or wine used in the recipe.

Nutmeg is most suitably used fresh and grated to capture its sweet, nutty flavour.

Pepper (ground) A black, rather sharp, hot-tasting spice. For a more subtle pepper flavour use white pepper.

Salt Some recipes call for a pinch of salt. A small pinch is about 1/8 teaspoon and a large pinch is about 1/4 teaspoon. Salt can enhance and sharpen the flavour of a lot of ingredients, but be careful not to overuse it. Aim to cut back, don't use it at every mealtime and use herbs a little more frequently to experience a wide range of flavours, beyond using salt alone. Note: excessive consumption of salt in our diet occurs when we excessively use canned, processed, takeaway and cured foods, where salt comes in hidden forms and amounts.

Sichuan Paste is a commercially prepared product that combines a whole lot of ingredients like tomato paste, chilli, soy sauce, vegetable oil, rice wine, fermented black beans, garlic, rice wine vinegar, oyster sauce, fermented soya beans and ginger in one small jar. It has a wonderful, warm, spicy Asian flavour that adds sensational taste to stirfries and noodle dishes.

Wasabi Powder A traditional spice of Japan, most often used in recipes like sushi and sashimi. It is a warm to hot spice, very much like horseradish. If using it in powder form, mix to a paste with a little water before adding it to the recipe.

Sun-dried Tomatoes are available in a dried form or marinated in a good olive oil. They are high in salt. To enjoy their flavour, you only need a small amount. Rehydrate dried tomatoes in a little water, stock or wine or drain off oil before using in recipes.

Tahini is a creamy paste made by grinding sesame seeds. There are two varieties, hulled and unhulled. I prefer the hulled (where the outside husk of the sesame seed is removed before grinding), mainly for its lighter texture and taste. Tahini is high in protein and calcium and 70 per cent of its total energy comes from unsaturated fats. It has a unique peanut taste and is a highly regarded food in a vegetarian diet.

Stock There are commercial varieties available, but check they are low in added salt. It is easy to make your own vegetable stock at home. Also see Miso Stock and Vecon Stock (see pages 156–7).

Tomato Paste is a concentrated purée of tomatoes. You can make your own by peeling and seeding tomatoes, chopping them finely and cooking them until they reduce and thicken, or you can purchase commercial varieties. Look for salt-free or low-salt varieties.

Vecon is a rich, concentrated vegetable paste that is sold in jars at health food shops. A teaspoon of Vecon dissolved in a cup of liquid makes a delicious-tasting stock that can be added to soups, sauces, stirfries and noodle recipes (see page 156).

Vegetables

A vegetarian diet should never be dull or lacking in nourishment when we consider the incredible variety of vegetables we have to choose from nearly all year round. For optimum health, it is recommended that we eat at least five or more servings of different vegetables each day. These can be teamed with pasta, rice and pulses, and fresh herbs and spices will enhance the flavour to make all sorts of interesting and tasty vegetarian meals. Include vegetables such as artichokes, asparagus, beans (broad, french and runner beans), beetroot, broccoli, brussels sprouts, cabbage (red and green), capsicums (red and green), carrots, cauliflower, celeriac, celery, chillies, cucumber, eggplants, fennel, leeks, lettuce (many varieties), mushrooms (cultivated and dried varieties), onions, parsnips, peas, potatoes (lots of varieties to choose from), pumpkin, radishes, rhubarb, squashes, shallots, spinach, swedes, sweetcorn, sweet potatoes, tomatoes, turnips and zucchini.

Canned Vegetables It makes a lot of sense to keep a couple of cans of vegetables in your pantry. Although fresh is best, canned vegetables such as corn kernels, asparagus spears, baby mushrooms, water chest-nuts, baby corn, baby carrots and artichoke hearts can be both an excellent complement and an essential ingredient in some recipes. They also enable you to use these ingredients when they may be out of season or difficult to find. All you need do is discard the liquid they come packed in and rinse them under cold running water to get rid of most of the salt.

Vinegars

Mainly used for salad dressings and to flavour vegetables. You won't use much, so this is one ingredient worth spending some extra dollars on. Look for a good-quality white and mild red vinegar, a balsamic vinegar and a cider vinegar for extra sharpness.

Balsamic Vinegar is a vinegar made from unfermented Trebbiano grapes grown in the foothills of Modena, Italy. Its unique dark red-rust colour enlivens salads when used alone or with a good olive oil. Its individual rich flavour is the outcome of its age, the quality of the original wine from which it was made and the type of wood from which the barrel that stored the vinegar is made. It is a firm favourite on Italian tables and is becoming more widely used in all styles of cooking.

Cider Vinegar is made from fermenting apples. It has a sharp flavour due to its high acidic nature. Be careful not to overuse it, especially with salad ingredients that have their own strong flavours. I like it mainly on salads that contain fruits like pear and apple.

Rice Wine Vinegar is a Japanese fermented rice wine with a sharp flavour.

White Wine Vinegar is a delicately flavoured vinegar made from white wine. Like red wine vinegar its flavour depends on the original wine from which it is made. It is an ideal vinegar to use as a base for making your own herb, garlic, chilli and raspberry vinegars. All you need to do is heat the vinegar and pour it over your favourite flavouring ingredients that you have packed into a bottle. For the best flavours allow it to stand for as long as possible. Sometimes the flavour of your own homemade vinegar (made without oils) is all a tossed vegetable salad requires.

GLOSSARY OF COOKING TERMS

Al dente is a term usually used for cooking pasta and rice but also for vegetables. It means to cook a food until it is just tender, yet still retaining a little bite.

Bake refers to the cooking of food by placing it in a hot oven.

Beat is the action that combines and/or aerates ingredients. It can be done by hand, with electric beaters or in food processors. Some ingredients, such as egg whites, need gentle beating, while other ingredients may need rigorous beating. Always follow the recipe guidelines for beating to ensure a successful outcome.

Blanch To blanch raw vegetables, place them in boiling water, leave for just a few minutes depending on size, and remove. Immediately refresh by plunging them into iced water for a few minutes to cool completely, then drain. Alternatively, vegetables can be steam-blanched in the microwave. Blanching enhances vegetable colour, removes bitter taste, loosens the skin of some fruits and vegetables and retains a lovely crispness.

Bruise is a term that describes the partial crushing of foods such as garlic, ginger, peppercorns or nuts. Bruising can be done between the fingers, with the wooden handle of a large knife or with a mortar and pestle.

Chargrill (see pages 144–6).

Chop To cut food roughly into no particular shape or size. Use your own discretion.

Degorge This is a simple process of removing the bitter juices from an eggplant prior to cooking. It is not necessary to use this process with young eggplant as the bitter juices have not yet developed. Cut the eggplant as the recipe suggests. Place in a bowl and salt liberally. Cover and allow the eggplant to stand for at least 2 hours. Rinse under cold running water to remove salt and bitter juices. Dry well before cooking.

Dice The process of chopping fruits and vegetables into small, even cubes.

Dry Roast is to cook food by dry heat under the griller, in the oven or on the base of a non-stick pan over an open flame.

Fat-free Cook Often we use fat in the cooking process so food does not stick to the base of the pan. A little water, stock, fruit juice or wine can be used to cook food in its initial stages instead of fats and oils. A browning effect can be achieved by cooking foods in heavy-based cookware. Simply place food such as onions, leeks and mushrooms onto the cold dry surface of a heavy-based pan and cover with a lid. Turn on the heat and allow the food to cook slowly in its own natural oils or juices. It will cook and naturally brown without the need to add any fat or oil. For cookware that does not have a heavy base, wipe the surface of the pan with just a little cooking oil and do not cook the food at excessively high temperatures.

Fold A gentle action of bringing a mixing spoon through the mixture as you continuously rotate the mixing bowl.

Fresh The best cooking results are always achieved when you use the freshest ingredients. Dry ingredients such as flour should be stored in airtight containers and out of direct sunlight. Fruits and vegetables are best refrigerated to keep them fresh. Wrap fresh herbs in a tea towel and keep refrigerated in an airtight container.

Julienne To cut fruits or vegetables (such as apples, zucchini or carrots) into very thin matchstick strips.

Marinate To cover foods with a combination of wet or dry ingredients and allow them to stand for at least an hour to promote a more intense flavour.

Pinch usually refers to salt, pepper, dried herbs or spices and is a small amount that can be held between the fingertips.

Poach To cook foods in simmering liquid (water, wine, stock, juice).

Purée To blend food to a smooth paste.

Refresh To run hot food under cold water to retain its vibrant colour or its cooked *al dente* nature.

Roast To lightly wipe food with oil, place in a hot oven and cook until food is softened and browned.

Segments Even thin wedge-like slices of fruits such as orange, grapefruit, mango. Completely remove peel and visible pith from citrus fruits before slicing.

Serve is a term you will find at the end of each recipe. It suggests additional foods or recipes that will complement the dish. This is important in a vegetarian diet so that you combine the appropriate foods that work together to enhance the absorption of particular nutrients. (For example, the absorption of iron is enhanced with the addition of vitamin C, therefore it is a good idea to drink a fresh juice with your morning cereal.)

Scramble The process of stirring food over and over to break it into small particles as it cooks (see Tofu Scrambled Eggs, page 59).

Sift To aerate dry ingredients by working them through a fine wire-mesh sifter.

Simmer To cook food in a hot liquid which is just bubbling.

Steam Cook Food is placed on a rack above boiling liquid, where the steam penetrates and cooks the food without it coming into contact with the water. Food can also be steam cooked in a microwave oven.

Stirfry Place 2 tablespoons–¼ cup water in the base of a wok or deep pan. Bring to the boil. Add 1–2 teaspoons of your favourite oil (sesame, olive, safflower). Add vegetables, toss, cover and cook. Remove cover often and toss vegetables so that those on the bottom of the pan do not stew or stick to the base of pan.

Whisk To beat mixture in a continuous motion with a wire whisk until ingredients combine. Whisking egg whites aerates them and gives them volume.

We've all been guilty of grabbing a piece of toast and a cup of coffee on the run or skipping breakfast altogether. Sometimes it's just too hard to think through the sleepy haze, let alone prepare a healthy meal, in the time available, for what is undoubtedly the most important meal of the day.

A vegetarian breakfast needs a little thought and planning if it is to get the motor started, provide the necessary fuel to keep the motor running and help the brain function for most of the day.

Variety is the key. Often I will use typical breakfast ingredients such as fresh fruit, eggs, yoghurt, soymilk, cereal, rolled oats, bread, sugar-free jam, dried fruits, nuts and seeds, fresh fruit and vegetable juices in ways that are not necessarily typically breakfast meals – in fact some would say they are more like a dessert!

At other times I might use unusual breakfast ingredients, such as cornmeal and tofu, and turn them into exciting, tasty, nutritional breakfast ideas that keep the whole family excited about waking up to the breakfast meal.

Breakfast Recipes

All these breakfast recipes follow the principles of a good healthy diet that is low in fat, high in fibre, loaded with fresh ingredients and provides lots of variety.

Apple and Walnut Pudding with Warm Apple Sauce

Serves 8–10

A warming recipe for when the last of the autumn leaves fall and it turns to winter, when the very smell of cooked apples and spices permeating through your kitchen is the perfect start to a cold day.

1 cup wholemeal plain flour
½ cup finely ground almonds
½ cup coarse cornmeal (polenta)
2 teaspoons baking powder
1 teaspoon cinnamon
3 Granny Smith apples, cored, chopped
2 tablespoons grapeseed oil
½ cup apple juice concentrate
¾ cup low-fat soymilk or low-fat milk
3 egg whites
icing sugar (optional garnish)

TOPPING
1 tablespoon grapeseed oil
2 tablespoons apple juice concentrate or honey
¼ cup walnuts
1 teaspoon cinnamon

APPLE SAUCE
4 Granny Smith apples, peeled, cored, sliced
1½ cups water
1 tablespoon lemon juice
2 tablespoons apple juice concentrate

- Preheat oven to 180°C and lightly oil a deep 6–8 cup capacity baking dish.
- Sift the first 5 ingredients into a large bowl, then add apple.
- In another bowl, combine grapeseed oil, apple juice concentrate, milk and egg whites and beat well.
- Gently fold into flour mixture.
- Spoon mixture into the baking dish. Combine topping ingredients and spoon over pudding.
- Bake for 1 hour or until top is brown and a skewer inserted into the centre of the pudding comes out clean.
- To make the sauce, combine all ingredients in a saucepan and simmer until apple is soft. Purée until smooth.

Serve hot from the oven, topped with warm Apple Sauce. Dust lightly with icing sugar as a garnish. It could also be served with low-fat Custard (see page 146) or Tofu Cream (see page 155). For a more filling meal, try this recipe with cooked fruit.

Apricot, Pear and Oat Crumble with Pear and Lemon Sauce

Serves 6–8

If you thought rolled oats were only a porridge food, this recipe will have you thinking again. Dust a little icing sugar over the warm crumble before serving.

PASTRY BASE
1 cup unbleached white plain flour
1 cup rolled oats
½ cup grapeseed oil
2 tablespoons apple juice concentrate
3 tablespoons orange juice

FILLING
1 x 825 g can unsweetened pears, well drained, chopped (reserve pear juice)
200 g dried apricots, diced

TOPPING
4 egg whites
2 tablespoons apple juice concentrate
1 cup finely ground almonds
½ cup finely ground hazelnuts
2 tablespoons rolled oats

PEAR and LEMON SAUCE
2 tablespoons cornflour
1½ cups unsweetened pear juice
1 tablespoon lemon juice
1 teaspoon finely grated lemon rind

- Preheat oven to 200°C. Line a non-stick 20 cm × 30 cm baking tray with paper.
- Combine all pastry ingredients in a food processor and blend until mixture binds together. Turn pastry out onto a floured bench and knead a little. Refrigerate for 30 minutes.
- Roll pastry to fit tray and press in. Bake for 15 minutes.
- To make the filling, combine pears and apricots and spread evenly over cooled pastry base.
- To make the topping, beat egg whites until stiff. While still beating, add apple juice concentrate, then gently fold in almonds and hazelnuts.
- Spoon mixture over pear and apricot mixture and then scatter over rolled oats.
- Reduce heat to 180°C and bake for 20–25 minutes or until golden brown.
- To make the sauce, mix cornflour with a little pear juice to make a paste. Place remaining pear juice, lemon juice and rind in a small saucepan and bring to the boil. Add paste and stir continuously until sauce boils and thickens.

Top warm crumble with Pear and Lemon Sauce and serve immediately.

Baked Summer Fruits with Passionfruit Syrup

Serves 4–6

Thank goodness for the wonderful flavour of passionfruit.

4 peaches, peeled, halved, stoned
4 nectarines, halved, stoned
4 apricots, halved, stoned
2 slices fresh pineapple, peeled, halved
2 mangoes, peeled, stoned, cut into large chunky pieces
1 cup cherries, stems removed, stoned

PASSIONFRUIT SYRUP
6–8 passionfruit
2 teaspoons finely grated orange rind
1 tablespoon apple juice concentrate or honey
¼ cup muscat or sweet sherry
¾ cup freshly squeezed orange juice

- Place prepared fruit except cherries in a shallow dish.
- Cut passionfruit in half, remove pulp and strain juice (reserve the seeds).
- Combine all the syrup ingredients, mixing well. Pour over the fruit and marinate for at least 1 hour before draining off the juice and reserving it.
- Lightly grill fruit on both sides until brown.
- Meanwhile, place marinade in a small saucepan and boil until it reduces to a syrup consistency.
- Add passionfruit seeds.
- Add cherries just to warm through.

Spoon a little of the syrup over the fruit and serve with low-fat yoghurt, low-fat vanilla frûche, low-fat Custard (page 146) or Tofu Cream (page 155). This recipe is also delicious served over warm cous cous or on top of porridge. Also serve with a breakfast of wholemeal toast and sugar-free jams or sprinkled with nuts and seeds.

Baked Ricotta with Balsamic Berries

Serves 6–8

This savoury breakfast dish is best eaten warm. The baked ricotta has a lovely soft texture, and a taste that complements the sweet and sharp flavours of fresh berries tinged with a hint of balsamic.

600 g low-fat ricotta cheese
2 teaspoons vanilla essence
1 kg mixed firm, fresh berries (blueberries, raspberries, blackberries, strawberries)
1 tablespoon lime juice
1 tablespoon balsamic vinegar
1 tablespoon honey, warmed

Variations

- For a lighter-textured baked ricotta, add 2 egg whites to ricotta cheese before blending.
- For a sweeter-tasting baked ricotta, add a little honey or apple juice concentrate to ricotta cheese before blending.
- Drizzle a little honey and sprinkle some cinnamon over the top of the ricotta about 15 minutes before it is completely cooked.

- Preheat oven to 180°C. Line a non-stick baking tray or a small springform cake tin with baking paper.
- Place ricotta and vanilla in a food processor and blend until smooth.
- Spoon onto baking tray and spread evenly to make a circle about 18 cm in diameter.
- Bake for 30 minutes or until the edges. and top begin to firm and brown lightly The ricotta will spread a little as it cooks. Allow to cool slightly.
- Combine berries (if using strawberries, remove green tops and cut fruit in half), lime juice, balsamic vinegar and warmed honey and allow to stand for 1 hour. Gently toss, being careful not to mush the berries.

Top the warm ricotta with berries and spoon over any remaining juices. Serve with fresh apple juice and a breakfast of wholemeal toast and sugar-free jams or topped with nuts and seeds.

Banana and Marsala Fruit and Honey Bread

Makes 10 slices

This is my 'stress-buster bread' because bananas are rich in norepinephrine and serotonin, nature's very own natural anti-depressants and feel-good substances. Bananas contain all the major vitamin groups and are packed with energy and fibre.

1½ cups dried mixed fruit (sultanas, currants, raisins, apricots, nectarines, peaches, apples)
¼ cup marsala
2 teaspoons cinnamon
1¼ cups unbleached white self-raising flour
¾ cup unbleached wholemeal self-raising flour
3 bananas, peeled, chopped
¼ cup grapeseed or carotino oil
½ cup honey, warmed
1¼ cups low-fat soymilk or low-fat milk
3 egg whites
¼ cup wheatgerm
extra cinnamon for garnish
icing sugar (optional garnish)

- Marinate dried fruit in marsala for at least 2 hours prior to making the recipe.
- Preheat oven to 180°C and line or lightly oil an 11 cm deep 28 cm × 12 cm bread tin.
- Sift cinnamon and flours into a bowl and add banana and marsala fruit.
- In another bowl, combine grapeseed oil, honey, milk and egg whites. Beat well.
- Gently fold into banana mixture.
- Spoon mixture into prepared tin, then scatter over wheatgerm.
- Bake for 40 minutes or until a skewer inserted into centre of cake comes out clean and top is golden brown.
- Remove to a cake stand, cover with a tea towel and allow to cool.
- Dust with combined cinnamon and icing sugar.

Serve hot from the oven topped with slices of fresh banana or cooked apple. Add some low-fat yoghurt, low-fat frûche, low-fat Custard (see page 146) or Tofu Cream (see page 155). The bread is also delicious served cold with a sugar-free marmalade or apricot jam.

Banana, Date and Ginger Pecan Muffins

Makes 8–12

These muffins are packed with the high-energy ingredients bananas, dates and nuts. Dates are an ideal vegetarian food containing lots of fibre and iron and a variety of other nutrients, such as vitamin B6, folate, niacin and magnesium.

3/4 cup wholemeal self-raising flour
1 1/4 cups unbleached self-raising flour
1/4 teaspoon mixed spice
1/4 teaspoon ground ginger
3 bananas, peeled, chopped
1 cup chopped dates
1 tablespoon finely chopped glacé ginger
1/2 cup chopped pecan nuts
1 tablespoon finely grated lemon or orange rind
1/4 cup grapeseed or carotino oil
1/2 cup apple juice concentrate
1 cup low-fat soymilk or low-fat milk
3 egg whites or 2 whole eggs
12 whole pecan nuts
icing sugar (optional garnish)

- Preheat oven to 180°C and lightly oil a muffin tray.
- Sift flours, mixed spice and ginger into a bowl. Add banana, dates, glacé ginger, pecan nuts and lemon rind.
- In another bowl, combine the grapeseed oil, apple juice concentrate, milk and egg whites and beat well.
- Add to banana mixture and mix well.
- Spoon into tray, topping each muffin with a whole pecan nut. Bake for 20–25 minutes or until tops are golden brown.
- Remove muffins onto a dry, clean tea towel or cake rack.

Serve hot from the oven garnished with a little icing sugar. You can make more of a meal with muffins by serving them with hot low-fat Custard (see page 146) or Tofu Cream (see page 155). Also serve with a freshly squeezed orange juice or a platter of fresh fruits that are high in vitamin C, such as berries or citrus fruits.

Berry Breakfast Clafouti

Serves 4–6

A fast, easy breakfast suggestion for those who love to sit down to a warm, wholesome breakfast after the morning ritual of stretching, walking or meditating.

2 whole eggs
2 tablespoons apple juice concentrate
½ cup low-fat soymilk, low-fat milk, buttermilk or almond milk (see page 144)
1 tablespoon vanilla essence
1½ cups unbleached plain white flour
300 g raspberries (fresh or frozen)
300 g blackberries (fresh or frozen)
icing sugar (optional garnish)

- Preheat oven to 180°C. Lightly oil a 5 cm deep × 25 cm round baking dish
- Combine all ingredients except berries in a food processor and mix to a smooth batter.
- Pour the batter into the baking dish.
- Scatter the berries over the top.
- Bake for 35–40 minutes (a little longer if using frozen fruit) or until clafouti is puffed, lightly browned on top and firm to touch.
- Remove from oven and dust lightly with a little icing sugar.

Serve with low-fat yoghurt, low-fat frûche, low-fat Custard (see page 146) or Tofu Cream (see page 155). Also serve with freshly squeezed orange juice.

Opposite: Baked Ricotta with Balsamic Berries (see page 35)

Serves 4

Berry Breakfast Pudding

Berries are loaded with fibre and plenty of nutrition. Add some high-fibre bread and there is nothing more delightful for breakfast than a traditional summer berry pudding.

1 cup water
3 tablespoons apple juice concentrate
½–1 teaspoon agar powder (see page 5)
1.5 kg mixed berries (blueberries, raspberries, mulberries, blackberries, redcurrants), fresh or frozen
16 slices white high-fibre bread, crusts removed
fresh berries for garnish

- Place water, apple juice concentrate and agar powder in a saucepan and slowly bring to the boil, stirring continuously to dissolve the agar.
- Stir in berries and gently cook until they begin to release their colour and juices.
- Cut each slice of bread in half. Line the base and sides of an 8-cup capacity pudding basin with some of the bread, overlapping slightly to make sure there are no gaps.
- Pour a large spoonful of berry juice over the base and allow it to soak into the bread before adding the remaining berry mixture.
- Cover the berries with the rest of the bread slices.
- Cover pudding with plastic wrap. Place a large plate on top and weigh it down with a heavy object.
- Refrigerate for at least 4–6 hours before slicing.

Serve with extra fresh berries in season and low-fat yoghurt or Tofu Cream (see page 155). Also serve with freshly squeezed orange juice or fresh apple juice.

Opposite: Polenta with Grilled Tomatoes and Mushrooms (see page 51)

Blueberry, Apple and Macadamia Muffins

Makes 8–12

It's amazing how such a small fruit as the blueberry can provide so much flavour. In this recipe it combines well with the wonderful, rich, almost buttery flavour of the macadamia nut.

1½ cups unbleached white self-raising flour
½ cup unbleached wholemeal plain flour
¾ cup finely chopped macadamia nuts
200 g blueberries (fresh or frozen)
250 g unsweetened cooked apple, roughly chopped
1 tablespoon finely grated lemon or orange rind
¼ cup grapeseed or carotino oil
½ cup apple juice concentrate
1 cup low-fat soymilk or low-fat milk
3 egg whites
icing sugar (optional garnish)

- Preheat oven to 180°C and lightly oil a muffin tray.
- Sift flours into a large bowl.
- Add macadamia nuts, blueberries, apple and rind.
- In another bowl, combine grapeseed oil, apple juice concentrate, milk and egg whites and beat well.
- Add to fruit and nut mixture and combine well.
- Spoon mixture into the muffin tray and bake for 20–25 minutes or until tops are golden brown.
- Turn out onto a dry, clean tea towel or cake rack.

Serve hot from the oven and garnish with a light dusting of icing sugar. You can make more of a meal with muffins by serving them with hot low-fat Custard (see page 146), Tofu Cream (see page 155) or a fruit sauce such as Lemon Sauce, Apricot Sauce or Orange Citrus Sauce (see pages 63, 154). Also serve with freshly squeezed orange juice or fresh apple juice.

Breakfast Fruit and Nut Smoothie

Serves 1

With a blender and the right ingredients you can create a sensational-tasting smoothie in no time at all that is power packed with nutrients, fibre and energy. If you haven't acquired a taste for soymilk, substitute low-fat milk, oat milk or almond milk (see page 144).

250 ml low-fat soymilk, well chilled
1 tablespoon rolled oats
½ unpeeled apple, cored, chopped
½ banana, peeled, chopped
1 small mandarin, peeled, pips removed
2–4 fresh dates, stoned or 4 dried apricots
2 tablespoons macadamia nuts or almonds
2 teaspoons apple juice concentrate or honey
pinch of nutmeg (optional)

Variation
For a creamier, protein-rich option add some silken tofu (see page 18). Sensational.

- Place all ingredients except nutmeg in a blender and blend until thick and creamy.

Serve in a tall glass, sprinkled with nutmeg.

Breakfast Oat, Fruit and Nut Cookies

Makes 12 large cookies

If you eat breakfast on the run, then this is the recipe for you. It's high in fibre, low in saturated fat, and contains everything you would find in a good bowl of cereal. With a glass of soymilk and a piece of fruit, this is an excellent start to a healthy day.

1 cup unbleached white plain flour
2 teaspoons baking powder
1 teaspoon mixed spice
1 teaspoon cinnamon
2 cups rolled oats
1 cup raisins (or any other dried fruit such as sultanas, currants, apricots or a mix of these)
¼ cup sunflower seeds
½ cup chopped mixed nuts (almonds, pecans, walnuts, peanuts, macadamias or cashews)
¼ cup pumpkin kernels
½ cup grapeseed or carotino oil
½ cup apple juice concentrate
2 egg whites

- Preheat oven to 180°C. Line a non-stick baking tray with paper.
- Sift flour, baking powder and spices into a large bowl. Add rolled oats, raisins, seeds and nuts.
- In another bowl, combine grapeseed oil, apple juice concentrate and egg whites and beat well.
- Add to oat mixture and mix well to make a sticky cookie mixture.
- Place spoonfuls onto baking tray.
- Bake for 20–25 minutes.
- Remove cookies immediately from baking tray and allow to cool on a wire rack.
- When cool, store cookies in an airtight jar.

Serve with a glass of soymilk or almond milk and a piece of fresh fruit such as banana, apple, pear, orange or mandarin.

Buckwheat Pancakes with Bananas and Blueberry Sauce

Serves 6

I am a huge fan of the humble blueberry. It is not only loaded with taste, but is an excellent source of vitamin C and a moderate source of iron and fibre. The combination flavours of blueberries, bananas and buckwheat is perfect.

PANCAKES
1 cup buckwheat flour
½ cup unbleached wholemeal self-raising flour
1 whole egg
1 egg white
1 tablespoon honey
1½ cups low-fat soymilk, low-fat milk or buttermilk
6 bananas, peeled, chopped

BLUEBERRY SAUCE
2 cups water
¼ cup cornflour
½ cup apple juice concentrate
600 g blueberries, fresh or frozen

Variation
Instead of Blueberry Sauce try Orange Citrus Sauce, Lemon Sauce or Apricot Sauce (see pages 63, 154).

- Place all pancake ingredients except bananas in a food processor and blend until smooth. Allow to stand for 30 minutes before cooking.
- Pour small amounts of pancake mixture onto a lightly oiled non-stick pan and cook until bubbles appear in the centre and the edges are slightly browned. Turn over and brown the other side.
- Repeat until all pancakes are cooked. Stir pancake mixture often and in between cooking each pancake. Remove cooked pancakes from pan and keep warm.
- To make the sauce, mix a little of the water with cornflour to make a paste. Place remaining water, apple juice concentrate and blueberries in a saucepan and slowly bring to the boil, stirring continuously. Carefully stir in cornflour paste and cook until sauce returns to the boil and thickens.

Top pancakes with chopped banana and spoon Blueberry Sauce over. Also serve with freshly squeezed orange juice or fresh apple juice.

Cornmeal Pancakes with Hot Fruit and Honey Syrup

Serves 6

If you've never tasted cornmeal before, this is a good introduction. It adds colour and a mealy texture and is a good source of thiamine and iron. Save this recipe for the weekend when you can take your time to enjoy the cooking experience as well as the eating.

PANCAKES

¾ cup coarse cornmeal (polenta)
1 cup unbleached plain white flour
2 teaspoons baking powder
1½ cups freshly squeezed orange juice
2 whole eggs
2 egg whites
6 cups chopped fresh, firm fruit (unpeeled apple, pineapple, mango, strawberries, blueberries, cherries, nectarines, peaches)

HONEY SYRUP

2 cups freshly squeezed orange juice
2 teaspoons finely grated lemon rind
¼ cup honey
1 teaspoon cinnamon or mixed spice

- Place all pancake ingredients except fruit in a food processor and blend until smooth. Allow to stand for 30 minutes before cooking.
- Pour some mixture into a lightly oiled non-stick pan and cook until bubbles appear in the centre and the edges are slightly browned. Turn over and brown the other side.
- Repeat until all pancakes are cooked. Stir pancake mixture often and in between cooking each pancake. Remove cooked pancakes from pan and keep warm.
- To make the syrup, place all ingredients in a small saucepan and bring to the boil. Turn heat down, simmer and reduce by half.
- Place fruit in a bowl and pour syrup over it.

Top pancakes with fruit and Honey Syrup. Also serve with fresh apple or pineapple juice.

Date and Nut Rolled Oat Bars

Serves 8

This recipe is a definite iron booster – particularly good for women on the run. It is sweetened with that most nutritious of foods – the date. Serve the bars plain, with low-fat yoghurt or Tofu Cream *(see page 155)**.*

PASTRY BASE

2 cups unbleached white plain flour
2 cups rolled oats
½ cup grapeseed or carotino oil
¼ cup apple juice concentrate
¼ cup freshly squeezed orange juice
¼ cup freshly squeezed lemon juice

DATE and NUT FILLING

1 tablespoon cornflour
2 cups freshly squeezed orange juice
300 g dates, stoned, finely chopped
1 teaspoon finely grated orange rind
1 cup macadamia nuts, halved

- Preheat oven to 180°C. Line a deep 20 cm × 30 cm baking tray with non-stick baking paper.
- Combine pastry ingredients in a food processor and blend.
- Divide pastry into two balls, wrap in plastic and chill for 30 minutes.
- Roll out each ball of pastry to make two rectangular shapes to fit in tray. Set aside to chill.
- To make the filling, combine the cornflour with 1 tablespoon of the orange juice to make a paste.
- Place dates, orange juice, and orange rind in a saucepan and slowly bring to the boil. Simmer gently for 15 minutes or until dates are soft.
- Add cornflour mixture and stir continuously until mixture thickens. Remove from heat, add macadamia nuts and allow mixture to cool.
- Press one piece of pastry firmly into baking tray.
- Bake for 15 minutes and allow to cool.
- Spread cooled date mixture over cooked pastry base and cover with the second piece of pastry. Using a fork, make some air holes in the top of the pastry. Bake for a further 20 minutes.
- Cool in tray before cutting into squares.

Fabulous Fruit Salad with Acidophilus Yoghurt and Passionfruit

Serves 4–6

Enjoy every mouthful of this fruit salad as the bittersweet, exotic flavours explode in your mouth. The acidophilus yoghurt, which contains lots of healthy bacteria, will restore the balance of healthy.

1 pawpaw, peeled, seeded, cubed
3 mangoes, peeled, stoned, cubed
2 bananas, peeled, sliced
1 avocado, peeled, stoned, cubed
1 small pineapple, peeled, cored, cubed
1 cup each of raspberries, blueberries and blackberries
juice of lime
1 cup low-fat plain acidophilus yoghurt
8 passionfruit, halved, pulp removed

- Combine all fruit except passionfruit with lime juice and stand for 1 hour.
- Pour yoghurt around the outside edge of the fruit. Spoon a little passionfruit pulp into the yoghurt and use a wooden skewer to run the passionfruit through the yoghurt decoratively.

Serve with freshly squeezed orange juice or fresh apple juice. This salad is also delicious served with flaked almonds, grated raw coconut, pumpkin seeds and sunflower seeds.

Fruity Cous Cous with Coconut Milk

Serves 4–6

Cous cous is a substitute for rice, which would be typically used in this recipe. It has the advantage over rice in that it takes only minutes to cook. Originally from North Africa, this rather versatile grain teams well with dried fruits and spices.

500 g cous cous
2 cups boiling water
1 tablespoon finely grated lemon rind
½ teaspoon cinnamon
1 tablespoon apple juice concentrate or honey, warmed
½ cup chopped dried apricots
2 tablespoons currants
2 tablespoons chopped dried figs
2 tablespoons chopped dried peaches, nectarines or pears
½ cup slivered almonds, toasted
2 tablespoons sunflower seeds
2 tablespoons pumpkin seeds
1 tablespoon sesame seeds, toasted
3–4 cups low-fat soymilk or low-fat milk, well chilled
1 x 140 ml can low-fat coconut milk, well chilled

- Pour boiling water over cous cous and mix well. Cover and let stand until cous cous swells and absorbs all the water. Toss lightly with a fork to separate the grains.
- Add remaining ingredients except milks and mix well.
- Combine milks and add to cous cous mixture.

Serve with freshly squeezed orange juice or fresh apple juice.

Oat Porridge with Grilled Honey Bananas and Yoghurt

Serves 4

If you've never eaten porridge before, then you are not only missing out on one of the healthiest of breakfast options, but in this case possibly one of the tastiest. This meal will provide you with more than enough fibre and fuel to accomplish any task.

2 cups rolled oats
pinch of salt (optional)
4 cups water
1 teaspoon finely grated lemon rind
4–6 bananas, peeled, sliced

HONEY SYRUP
½ cup freshly squeezed orange juice
2 tablespoons honey
½ teaspoon cinnamon

- Combine rolled oats, salt, water and lemon rind in a saucepan and stir well, cover and cook slowly until mixture begins to boil. Give mixture a good stir, turn heat down and cook for a further 5 minutes until porridge begins to thicken. Turn off heat and leave covered.
- To make the syrup, place orange juice, honey and cinnamon in a small pan and bring to the boil. Reduce heat and simmer until reduced by half. Remove from heat.
- Add banana and coat with syrup, but remove before fruit softens. Place under a griller to brown.

Serve topped with low-fat yoghurt or low-fat frûche slices of grilled banana. Drizzle any remaining juices over the porridge. Also serve with fresh apple or pineapple juice.

Peach and Marmalade Breakfast Bread Pudding

Serves 4–6

Peaches and marmalade were meant to be together. This recipe simply proves my theory!

- 8–12 fresh yellow peaches, peeled, halved, stoned (canned unsweetened peaches can be used if fresh peaches are not obtainable)
- 8 slices white high-fibre bread
- ¾ cup sugar-free marmalade (available from supermarkets and health food shops)
- 2 cups low-fat soymilk or low-fat milk
- ¼ cup cornflour
- 2 tablespoons apple juice concentrate or honey
- 2 whole eggs or 3 egg whites
- 1 tablespoon vanilla essence
- icing sugar (optional garnish)

- Place peaches in a saucepan, cover with water and gently poach until soft. Drain well. If using canned peaches do not cook, but drain well.
- Preheat the oven to 170°C. Lightly oil a 4 cm deep 28 cm × 20 cm baking dish.
- Spread slices of bread with marmalade and cut each piece in half. Place a layer of bread on base of baking dish and top with peaches.
- Beat together all the remaining ingredients except bread and pour over peaches. Top with another layer of bread and press down.
- Bake for 30–40 minutes or until pudding is golden brown.

Serve warm with low-fat yoghurt, low-fat Custard (see page 146) or Tofu Cream (see page 155) and garnish with a little icing sugar. Also serve with fresh apple or pineapple juice.

Pear and Almond Clafouti

Serves 6

Almost too good to be a breakfast dish, but then, why not?

6 egg whites
⅓ cup apple juice concentrate
2 teaspoons almond essence
200 g finely ground almonds
½ cup unbleached white self-raising flour
1 tablespoon finely grated orange rind
500 g cold, cooked unsweetened pears
icing sugar (optional garnish)

- Preheat oven to 180°C. Lightly oil a 5 cm deep 25 cm round baking dish.
- Beat egg whites until stiff. Continue beating and slowly add apple juice concentrate and almond essence.
- Combine ground almonds, flour and orange rind and fold into egg whites with a spoon.
- Pour batter into baking dish. Place pears in a circular pattern on top of batter.
- Bake for 40–50 minutes or until clafouti is puffed, lightly browned and firm.
- Remove from oven and cut into wedges.

Serve hot clafouti with slices of fresh apple or pineapple, low-fat yoghurt, low-fat frûche, low-fat Custard (see page 146) or Tofu Cream (see page 155) and garnish with a little icing sugar. Also serve with freshly squeezed orange juice.

Polenta with Grilled Tomatoes and Mushrooms

Serves 4–6

In northern Italy polenta is a staple food served either soft or set firm and grilled to accompany vegetables and salads. Its taste and texture are unique and, in this recipe, it makes a perfect substitute for toast.

1 cup coarse cornmeal (polenta)
pinch of salt
2 cups water
olive oil
4–6 grilled tomatoes (see page 151)
8–12 large chargrilled mushrooms (see page 146)

DRESSING
2 teaspoons olive oil
1 tablespoon balsamic vinegar
1 tablespoon finely chopped fresh basil
freshly ground black pepper
extra basil leaves for garnish

- Line a 26 cm × 14 cm baking dish with baking paper.
- Combine cornmeal, salt and water in a saucepan and slowly bring to the boil, stirring continuously, until polenta begins to thicken and comes away from the sides of the saucepan.
- Spread polenta in baking dish and refrigerate until firm.
- Cut into 4–6 squares. Wipe back and front of each square with just a little olive oil and grill on both sides until crisp and lightly browned.
- Combine dressing ingredients, adding any leftover cooked tomato and mushroom juices.

Serve polenta squares topped with tomatoes and mushrooms. Spoon dressing over polenta and garnish with fresh basil leaves. Also serve with fresh carrot and capsicum juice.

Pumpkin and Honey Bread

Makes 12 slices

The pumpkin is the secret ingredient in this bread, adding moisture and sweetness and a lovely orange colour. The honey and spices are the added bonus. For variation you could substitute sweet potato for the pumpkin.

1½ cups unbleached white self-raising flour
½ cup unbleached wholemeal self-raising flour
1 teaspoon ground ginger
2 teaspoons cinnamon
1½ cups raisins
600 g cold cooked pumpkin, mashed
¼ cup grapeseed or carotino oil
½ cup honey
1¼ cups low-fat soymilk, low-fat milk, buttermilk or almond milk (see page 144)
1 whole egg
2 egg whites
2 tablespoons pumpkin seeds (optional)

- Preheat oven to 180°C. Lightly oil and line an 11 cm deep 28 cm × 12 cm bread tin.
- Sift the flours and spices into a large bowl. Add the raisins and pumpkin.
- In another bowl, combine the grapeseed oil, honey, milk and eggs and beat well. Add to pumpkin mixture and mix well.
- Spoon into bread tin and scatter pumpkin seeds over. Bake for 50 minutes or until a skewer inserted in the centre of the bread comes out clean.
- Remove bread immediately from tin and cool on a cake rack before cutting into thick slices.

Serve topped with cooked apple and low-fat yoghurt, low-fat Custard (see page 146), Tofu Cream (see page 155) or Pear and Lemon Sauce (see page 39). Also serve with a freshly squeezed orange juice.

Makes 12 slices

Raisin and Apple Bread

The delicious flavours of raisins and cinnamon are wonderfully enhanced in this recipe with a hint of apple.

1 cup unbleached self-raising flour
1 cup wholemeal plain flour
2 teaspoons baking powder
1½ teaspoons cinnamon
1 cup raisins
1 cup grated apple, firmly packed
3 tablespoons low-fat yoghurt
1 cup low-fat soymilk or low-fat milk

- Preheat oven to 180°C. Line a non-stick baking tray with paper.
- Sift flours, baking powder and cinnamon into a bowl.
- Add raisins, apple, yoghurt and milk and mix to a sticky dough.
- Turn dough onto a lightly floured bench and knead.
- Shape dough into a long loaf shape and place on baking tray. With a sharp knife make two shallow cuts across the top.
- Bake for 25–30 minutes or until the crust is brown and the loaf sounds hollow when tapped.
- Remove from tin and wrap in a tea towel and allow to cool before slicing and toasting.

Serve plain or with low-fat cottage or low-fat ricotta cheese and sugar-free jam.

Risotto with Apple, Raisins and Almonds

Serves 4

Risotto is a perfect breakfast, lunch or dinner meal. If you feel adventurous you can change the recipe as you go, depending on the ingredients you have on hand. The secret to a good risotto is to maintain a constant, not-too-hot pan temperature and stir continuously.

1 cup arborio rice
3 cups freshly squeezed orange juice
1 teaspoon cinnamon
1 tablespoon finely grated lemon rind
100 ml white wine
2 large Granny Smith apples, cored, cubed
½ cup raisins
¼ cup slivered almonds
extra raisins and slivered almonds for garnish

- Place first 4 ingredients in a cold, heavy-based pan. Heat pan and slowly cook, stirring continuously, until nearly all liquid is absorbed.
- Add wine, apple and raisins and stir. Cover and cook until apple is soft but not mushy. You may need to stir occasionally to prevent the fruit sticking to the base of the pan.
- Just before serving, stir in almonds.

Garnish risotto with a few extra raisins and slivered almonds. Also serve with freshly squeezed orange and pineapple juice.

Risotto with Dried Fruit Compote

Serves 4

An old-fashioned fruit compote with a new, creamy rice twist. Dried pears and dried figs are an excellent source of iron.

1 cup arborio rice
3 cups low-fat milk or low-fat soymilk
1 tablespoon grated orange rind
1 tablespoon vanilla essence
½ teaspoon nutmeg

DRIED FRUIT COMPOTE
100 g dried apricots
100 g dried pears, halved
100 g dried nectarines
200 g dried figs, halved
100 g prunes, stoned
1 teaspoon cinnamon
½ teaspoon mixed spice
2 cups freshly squeezed orange juice
½ cup brandy, muscat or port
1 tablespoon finely grated orange rind

- To make the compote, combine all ingredients in a saucepan. Simmer, uncovered, for approximately 10 minutes or until fruit has just softened.
- Remove fruit from cooking juices and keep warm.
- Boil remaining juice until reduced by half.
- Return cooked fruit to what should now be a syrup and keep warm while you cook the risotto.
- To cook risotto, place all ingredients in a cold, heavy-based pan. Heat and slowly cook, stirring continuously, until all liquid is absorbed and rice is tender but still holds its shape.

Serve risotto topped with the compote. Also serve freshly squeezed orange juice.

Semolina Porridge with Marsala Fruits

Serves 4–6

Semolina mixed with rolled oats produces a soft, creamy porridge, and the combination of two grains provides a more complete protein for a vegetarian diet.

1 cup durum semolina
1 cup rolled oats
pinch of salt (optional)
6 cups cold water

MARSALA FRUITS
100 g dried apricots
100 g dried pears, cut into strips
100 g dried nectarines
1 tablespoon grated lemon rind
1 tablespoon grated orange rind
1 teaspoon cinnamon
¼ teaspoon mixed spice
2 cups freshly squeezed orange juice
1 tablespoon freshly squeezed lemon juice
¼ cup marsala
100 g dried figs
1 Granny Smith apple, cored, sliced
1 pear, cored, sliced

- To make the marsala fruits, place all ingredients in a saucepan and bring to the boil. Reduce heat and simmer until all fruit is just soft.
- Remove fruit from liquid and keep warm. Boil remaining juices until reduced by half and return softened fruit to saucepan. Remove from heat.
- Place semolina, oats, salt and water in a small saucepan. Stir continuously until porridge begins to bubble and thicken. Reduce heat a little and keep stirring so porridge does not stick to the base of the pan. If it is too thick, add a little more cold water.

Serve immediately, topped with marsala fruits. This is delicious with a little low-fat yoghurt, low-fat frûche or low-fat soymilk. Also serve with freshly squeezed orange juice.

Simple Cinnamon and Soy Pancakes with Mango and Figgy Maple Syrup

Serves 4–6

There's not a lot of fibre in these soft, fluffy pancakes, but the fibre in the mango and dried figs makes up for it.

1 cup unbleached plain white flour
2 teaspoons baking powder
1 teaspoon cinnamon
1 cup low-fat soymilk
1 whole egg
1 egg white
3–4 mangoes

FIGGY MAPLE SYRUP
½ cup chopped dried figs
2 tablespoons freshly squeezed lemon juice
2 tablespoons freshly squeezed orange juice
¼ teaspoon mixed spice
½ cup maple syrup
½ cup water

- Place flour, baking powder, cinnamon, soymilk and eggs in a food processor and mix to a smooth batter.
- Pour small amounts of mixture into a lightly oiled non-stick pan and cook until bubbles appear in the centre and the edges are slightly browned. Turn over and brown the other side.
- Repeat until you have cooked all the pancakes. Stir mixture often and in between cooking each pancake. Remove cooked pancakes from pan and keep warm.
- To make the syrup, combine all ingredients in a small pan and bring to the boil. Reduce heat and simmer until mixture reduces and becomes quite syrupy. Cool slightly.
- Peel mangoes and slice.

Top each serving with mango slices and spoon syrup over. Serve with low-fat frûche or Tofu Cream (see page 155). Also serve with freshly squeezed orange and mandarin juice.

Sweet Potato Pie

Serves 4–6

The goodness of sweet potato is teamed here with warm aromatic spices that are typically American in style and flavour.

- 800 g cold cooked sweet potato, mashed
- 200 g coarsely ground almonds
- 1 teaspoon cinnamon
- ½ teaspoon nutmeg
- ½ teaspoon ground ginger
- 1 tablespoon finely grated orange rind
- 1 tablespoon dry sherry or marsala
- 1 x 140 ml can low-fat coconut milk
- 1 cup low-fat soymilk or low-fat milk
- ½ cup apple juice concentrate or honey
- 2 egg whites, lightly beaten
- 500 g blueberries

- Preheat oven to 180°C. Lightly oil a 4 cm deep 28 cm × 20 cm non-stick baking dish, or line with paper.
- Combine all ingredients except blueberries in the order that they are listed. Mix well.
- Spread the mixture evenly in baking dish.
- Cook for 50–60 minutes or until top is brown and the centre of pie is firm to touch.
- Remove from oven and allow to cool in baking dish before slicing.

Serve with low-fat yoghurt, low-fat Custard (see page 146) or Tofu Cream (see page 155) and garnish with fresh blueberries.

Serves 2–4

Tofu Scrambled Eggs

If you need to keep your cholesterol in check, you don't have to give up the wonderful flavour of an old-time favourite – scrambled eggs. This recipe substitutes tofu for the egg yolks. With a little turmeric to give you a rich yellow colour, you will hardly notice the difference.

350 g silken tofu (see page 18)
4 egg whites
1 teaspoon turmeric
pinch of salt (optional)
freshly ground black pepper
2 tablespoons finely chopped parsley
2 tablespoons finely chopped chives

- Drain and mash tofu.
- Lighly mix egg whites and turmeric in a blender.
- Lightly combine tofu and egg mixture. Place mixture in a hot, lightly oiled, non-stick frying pan and continually turn mixture over until it becomes firm.
- Add salt, pepper and herbs.

Serve on wholemeal toast or on a bed of chargrilled vegetables (eggplants, tomatoes, mushrooms and capsicums: see pages 144–6). Also serve with freshly squeezed orange juice.

Tropical Muesli

Makes 1.5 kg (6 cups)

Making your own muesli is fun and allows you to add your favourite ingredients. Use this recipe as a guide and then make up your own. You'll find all sorts of interesting and tasty ingredients at your local supermarket and health food shop.

2 cups puffed brown rice
2 cups processed rice bran
2 cups triticale flakes
2 cups barley flakes
200 g dried pawpaw pieces
200 g dried pineapple pieces
200 g sultanas
¼ cup sunflower seeds
¼ cup pumpkin seeds

- Combine all ingredients in a large bowl and mix well.
- Store muesli in an airtight jar.

Serve with low-fat soymilk, low-fat milk or almond milk, chopped fresh fruit or cooked, unsweetened fruit.

Serves 1

Vegie Tofu Smoothie

A healthy breakfast can be made quickly and without much fuss by simply going to your vegetable crisper and juicing whatever is on hand. If you haven't got the following vegetables, don't worry – most vegetable combinations work.

100 g beetroot
200 g carrot
100 g celery
100 g red capsicum, seeded
80 g–100 g silken tofu
(see page 18)

Variations

- Add some red chilli for a fiery start to the day (increases metabolism).
- Add some fresh ginger (improves digestion).
- Add some fresh garlic (keeps the colds away).
- Add a teaspoon of flaxseeds or sesame seeds for a nutty, chewy texture (both add valuable and necessary omega fatty acids to the diet).
- For extra fibre, add a spoonful of the fibrous vegetable pulp to the smoothie and stir well before drinking (prevents and relieves constipation).
- Add some chopped fresh parsley (for extra taste).

- Chop vegetables and juice them.
- Place juice and tofu in a blender and blend until thick and creamy.

This smoothie is the perfect accompaniment to a breakfast of wholemeal toast topped with slices of tomato or avocado.

Wheat-free Berry, Banana and Apricot Muffins

Makes 12

If you need a wheat-free recipe that all the family will love, this is it. Even if wheat is not a problem in your diet, this recipe shows you how to use a wider variety of ingredients on a regular basis.

1 cup rice flour
⅓ cup soy flour
½ cup cornmeal (polenta)
2 teaspoons baking powder
½ teaspoon bicarbonate of soda
¼ teaspoon mixed spice
2 teaspoons cinnamon
250 g blueberries
2 bananas, peeled, chopped
100 g dried apricots, chopped
1 tablespoon finely grated lemon or orange rind
½ cup grapeseed or carotino oil
½ cup apple juice concentrate
¾ cup low-fat soymilk or low-fat milk
3 whole eggs or 4 egg whites
icing sugar (optional garnish)

- Preheat oven to 180°C and lightly oil a muffin tray.
- Sift the dry ingredients into a bowl.
- Add berries, bananas, apricots and rind.
- In another bowl, combine grapeseed oil, apple juice concentrate, milk and eggs and beat well.
- Add to banana mixture and combine.
- Spoon into muffin tray and bake for 20–25 minutes or until tops are golden brown.
- Remove muffins and cool.

Serve hot from the oven garnished with a little icing sugar. Also serve with freshly squeezed orange and pineapple juice.

Wheat-free Lemon, Apple and Spice Muffins with Lemon Sauce

Makes 12

The tangy lemon sauce makes these muffins just a little more special. You can serve the sauce warm or, if you allow it to cool, use it as a substitute to lemon butter.

1 cup rice flour
½ cup soy flour
⅓ cup cornmeal (polenta)
2 teaspoons baking powder
½ teaspoon bicarbonate of soda
1 teaspoon mixed spice
2 teaspoons cinnamon
1 x 425 g can unsweetened apples, chopped
2 tablespoons finely grated lemon rind
½ cup grapeseed or carotino oil
½ cup apple juice concentrate
¾ cup low-fat soymilk or low-fat milk
3 whole eggs or 4 egg whites
icing sugar (optional garnish)

LEMON SAUCE
1¼ cups water
¼ cup cornflour
¼ cup freshly squeezed lemon juice
½ cup apple juice concentrate
1 tablespoon finely grated lemon rind

- Preheat oven to 180°C and lightly oil a muffin tray.
- Sift dry ingredients into a large bowl. Add apple and lemon rind.
- In another bowl, combine grapeseed oil, apple juice concentrate, milk and eggs and beat well.
- Add to apple mixture and combine well.
- Spoon into muffin tray and bake for 20–25 minutes or until tops are golden brown.
- Remove muffins immediately from tray and allow to cool a little.
- To make the lemon sauce, mix a little water with the cornflour to make a paste.
- Combine the remaining water, lemon juice, apple juice concentrate and lemon rind in a small saucepan and bring to the boil. Stir in the cornflour paste and keep stiring until mixture boils and thickens.

Spoon warm Lemon Sauce over each muffin. You could also add some Tofu Cream (see page 155) or low-fat yoghurt.

I am assuming that, like me, you don't have lots of spare hours in the middle of the day to ponder and prepare a difficult and time-consuming recipe.

These vegetarian lunch recipes are designed to sustain and satisfy your appetite, with an understanding of your energy and nutritional needs to get you through the remainder of the day. However, we now know that it is inappropriate to eat a big lunch. A big lunch results in a sluggish afternoon with the body needing all its energy to digest the meal rather than stimulating brain and physical functions.

These lunch recipes are full of essential fibre, which is not only good for the bowel, it tends to fill you up, so you shouldn't crave more food during the afternoon.

Lunch Recipes

These recipes take advantage of our wonderful supply and variety of fresh fruits, vegetables and herbs, available all year around. Now, like never before, healthier fast-food ingredients are available at supermarkets and delis, to team with fresh foods for good-quality, light, no-fuss, healthy meals. You'll feel good because all these recipes are good for you. You'll enjoy the simple effort it takes to prepare something that looks so tempting and tastes terrific.

Baked Beany Potatoes with Pesto

Serves 4

A baked potato and a few pantry items makes a tasty, fast lunch. In this recipe, the beans and chickpeas provide essential iron for that 'get up and go' energy for the rest of the day and the low-fat yoghurt and salad greens add extra iron.

4 large potatoes, washed, dried
1 x 300 g can butter beans, well drained
1 x 300 g can chickpeas, well drained
½ firm, ripe avocado, peeled, chopped
½ cup finely chopped spring onions
1 cup finely chopped seeded cucumber
freshly ground black pepper
½ cup low-fat yoghurt, low-fat cottage cheese or mashed silken tofu (see page 18)
¼ cup Pesto (see page 152)

- Preheat oven to 200°C.
- Bake potatoes until they are crisp on the outside and soft on the inside.
- Meanwhile, combine butter beans, chickpeas, avocado, spring onion, cucumber and pepper.
- When potatoes are cooked, break open each one to create a pocket. Place a spoonful of yoghurt, cottage cheese or tofu into each potato. Top with bean mixture and a spoonful of Pesto.

Serve immediately with a green salad (see pages 150–151).

Baked Sweet Potato with Spinach and Tofu Salad

Serves 2

Sweet potatoes are quite different to their white cousins. Both have the same kilojoule value but the sweet potato contains more vitamins. They are loaded with vitamin A and are a good source of vitamin C, vitamin E, calcium and essential dietary fibre.

2 medium sweet potatoes, washed, dried
350 g firm tofu, cut into cubes or slices
200 g spinach, washed, well drained
1 tablespoon freshly chopped mint
1 tablespoon freshly chopped coriander
1 tablespoon finely chopped cashews
1 teaspoon sesame seeds
½ cup Spicy Oriental Dressing (see page 149)

- Preheat oven to 200°C.
- Bake sweet potatoes until they are crisp on the outside and soft on the inside.
- Grill tofu (see page 156).
- Combine spinach, herbs, cashews and sesame seeds. Gently fold in grilled tofu. Add dressing and toss lightly.
- When sweet potatoes are cooked, break open each one to create a pocket. Fill sweet potatoes with equal amounts of salad and spoon any remaining dressing over them.

Serve immediately. Also serve with fresh carrot and capsicum juice.

Beetroot Cake

Serves 10

This delicious, magenta-coloured cake is a wonderful surprise served as a savoury meal. Alternatively, try thick slices served with low-fat yoghurt and cinnamon as a dessert.

300 g beetroot, peeled, finely grated
200 g raisins
100 g walnuts, chopped
1¼ cups unbleached white self-raising flour
¾ cup unbleached wholemeal self-raising flour
1 teaspoon nutmeg
1 teaspoon cinnamon
½ cup apple juice concentrate or honey
1 cup low-fat soymilk or low-fat milk
1 whole egg
2 egg whites
2 tablespoons sesame seeds

- Preheat oven to 180°C. Line an 11 cm deep non-stick 28 cm × 12 cm bread tin with baking paper.
- Combine beetroot, raisins and walnuts in a large bowl. Sift in flours and spices.
- In another bowl, combine apple juice concentrate, milk and eggs and beat well. Gently fold into beetroot mixture.
- Spoon mixture into prepared tin and sprinkle top with sesame seeds.
- Bake for 45 minutes or until firm in the centre and golden brown on top.
- Remove to a cake rack and cool.

Serve warm with thin slices of fresh silken tofu and a green salad (see pages 150–1). Dress with balsamic vinegar and plenty of freshly ground black pepper.

Serves 10–12

Carrot Cake

This cake is packed with so much goodness it deserves to be considered as a lunch meal. It is an adaptation of the classic carrot cake recipe. I reason that a little bit of honey is okay if I'm prepared to give up the traditional cream-cheese icing!

300 g carrot, finely grated
200 g currants
½ cup chopped walnuts
1 cup unbleached white self-raising flour
1 cup unbleached wholemeal plain flour
½ teaspoon bicarbonate of soda
2 teaspoons cinnamon
½ cup grapeseed or carotino oil
½ cup honey
4 egg whites
1 tablespoon vanilla essence
10 extra walnuts

- Preheat oven to 180°C. Line an 11 cm deep non-stick 28 cm × 12 cm bread tin with baking paper.
- Combine carrot, currants and walnuts in a large bowl. Sift in dry ingredients.
- In another bowl, combine grapeseed oil, honey, egg whites and vanilla essence and beat well.
- Gently fold into carrot mixture.
- Spoon mixture into prepared tin and decorate with extra walnuts.
- Bake for 1 hour or until firm in the centre and golden brown on top.
- Remove to a cake stand and allow to cool.

Serve thick slices topped with low-fat yoghurt or Tofu Cream (see page 155). Add some slices of banana or cooked apple sprinkled with cinnamon or mixed spice. Also serve with freshly squeezed orange juice.

Caesar Salad

Serves 4–6

Not truly a vegetarian dish because of its use of fish sauce, but this ingredient is used minimally and imparts a major flavour to an all-time favourite salad – with much less fat than the original recipe.

400 g cos (romaine) lettuce leaves (choose inner, young green leaves)
½ loaf day-old white high-fibre bread or grain bread
1 tablespoon olive oil
1 tablespoon fish sauce
1 teaspoon crushed garlic
white of 6–8 hard-boiled eggs, roughly chopped
⅓ cup grated parmesan cheese
¼ cup finely chopped chives

DRESSING
1 cup low-fat yoghurt
1 tablespoon low-fat cholesterol-free mayonnaise (see page 22)
1 tablespoon apple juice concentrate
2 teaspoons – 1 tablespoon fish sauce (see page 18)
¼ teaspoon dry mustard
¼ teaspoon ground black pepper

- To make the dressing, place all ingredients in a glass jar and shake well. Use just 2 teaspoons of fish sauce at first and add more if you are looking for a saltier taste. There is fish sauce in the croutons, and after a few mouthfuls you can certainly taste its strong flavour, so use it sparingly.
- Wash lettuce leaves and dry thoroughly, breaking off any brown or tired-looking edges.
- Cut bread into slices, remove crusts and cut into cubes. Combine oil, fish sauce and garlic, pour over the bread and toss well. Spread croutons on a non-stick baking tray and bake at 180°C until golden brown, or toast on both sides under a griller.
- Combine croutons, lettuce, egg whites, parmesan and chives in a large bowl. Pour over dressing, toss and serve immediately.

This salad is delicious with chargrilled vegetables such as capsicums, mushrooms, eggplant, zucchini or carrots (see pages 144–6). Also serve with fresh carrot and capsicum juice.

Chickpea and Pumpkin Burgers with Cucumber Dip

Serves 6

These burgers are ideal for a light lunch. The key is not to overprocess the chickpeas, so you can enjoy the taste and the crunch.

2 x 300 g can chickpeas, well drained, rinsed
400 g pumpkin, cooked, drained, mashed
1 onion, finely diced
100 g red capsicum, seeded, finely diced
1 egg white
2 teaspoons finely chopped fresh ginger
1 teaspoon coriander
2 teaspoons cumin
1 teaspoon crushed garlic
½ cup chopped chives
6 wholemeal burger buns
1 cup shredded lettuce
1 cup grated carrot

CUCUMBER DIP

200 ml low-fat yoghurt or mashed silken tofu (see page 18)
1 tablespoon low-fat cholesterol-free mayonnaise (see page 22)
1 teaspoon crushed garlic
1 cup peeled, seeded, finely diced cucumber
1 tablespoon finely chopped fresh dill or mint
freshly ground black pepper

- Place chickpeas in a food processor and process until they resemble large breadcrumbs (do not overprocess).
- Place processed chickpeas in a bowl with vegetables, egg white and herbs. Mix well, then work mixture together in your hands until it begins to stick together.
- Shape into burgers and refrigerate for at least 1 hour before cooking. This will help them hold their shape during cooking.
- Wipe the base of a non-stick pan with a little olive oil and heat. When pan is hot, cook burgers on both sides until brown and crisp. Remove from pan and keep warm.
- To make the Cucumber Dip, combine all ingredients in a small bowl and mix well.
- Place each burger on half a burger bun. Top with some lettuce, carrot, Cucumber Dip and the other burger bun half.

Serve with freshly squeezed orange juice or carrot and capsicum juice.

Chickpea and Spinach Salad with Tahini and Vindaloo Dressing

Serves 4–6

This salad looks good and tastes crunchy – terrific.

2 chargrilled red capsicums, chopped (see page 144)
200 g green beans, cut into 4 cm lengths
200 g Lebanese cucumber, cut into rounds
600 g baby spinach, washed
1 red onion, finely diced
2 x 300 g can chickpeas, well drained, rinsed
½ cup currants, plumped in warm water
ground black pepper
½ cup chopped fresh parsley

TAHINI and VINDALOO DRESSING
1 teaspoon vindaloo curry paste (see page 20)
2 tablespoons tahini paste (see page 23)
2 teaspoons apple juice concentrate
½ cup freshly squeezed orange juice
1 tablespoon freshly squeezed lemon or lime juice
1–2 teaspoons finely chopped fresh coriander or mint

- Combine all salad ingredients in a bowl.
- In another bowl, combine all dressing ingredients and mix together well.
- Pour dressing over salad ingredients and toss lightly. Refrigerate for at least 1 hour to allow flavours to develop.

Scatter some sesame seeds over this salad for a tasty variation. Also serve with freshly squeezed orange juice or fresh carrot and capsicum juice.

Makes 12 slices

Country Grain and Soy Bread

I like to choose my own mix of organic flours and grains to make a very tasty loaf. I particularly like a heavy, moist bread with a crunchy crust. This one is delicious hot from the oven and makes sensational toast. It also looks and smells wonderful.

14 g dry yeast
1 tablespoon apple juice concentrate or honey
2 cups unbleached plain white flour
1½ cups unbleached plain wholemeal flour
½ cup soy flour
2 cups warm water
2 tablespoons sunflower seeds
2 tablespoons sesame seeds
½ cup cracked wheat

- Lightly oil an 11 cm deep 28 cm × 12 cm bread tin.
- Combine yeast, apple juice concentrate, sifted flours and water in a large mixing bowl. Using a bread hook on a food mixer, mix for 5 minutes.
- Add seeds and cracked wheat and continue kneading by hand or mixing with bread hook.
- Place dough into a lightly oiled bowl, cover and allow to stand for 30 minutes in a warm spot or until dough has more than doubled in size.
- Punch dough down and knead for a few minutes on a lightly floured bench. Fit into prepared tin. Cover with a cloth and again place in a warm spot for approximately 30 minutes or until dough has reached the top of the tin.
- Preheat oven to 230°C. Bake the loaf for 35–40 minutes or until crust is brown and makes a hollow sound when tapped.
- Remove bread from tin and wrap in a dry tea towel to cool before slicing.

Serve thick slices of bread topped with Eggplant Dip (see page 75), Three Bean Dip (see page 88) or Hot Guacamole (see page 87).

Dahl with Onion and Cheese Damper

Serves 4

A tasty, economical dish of Indian origins. It is a spicy, thick porridge-like meal made from split peas or lentils that can be served as a dip or, thinned with water or stock, as a soup.

1 cup yellow split peas, washed
5 cups water
1 onion, finely diced
1 teaspoon finely chopped fresh ginger
1 teaspoon crushed garlic
1 teaspoon cumin
¾ teaspoon mustard seeds
½ teaspoon turmeric
½ teaspoon garam masala
¼ teaspoon cinnamon
¼ teaspoon coriander
pinch of salt
½ cup finely chopped, seeded red capsicum
½ cup finely chopped carrot

ONION and CHEESE DAMPER
1 cup unbleached self-raising flour
1 cup wholemeal plain flour
2 teaspoons baking powder
1 tablespoon chopped chives
1 tablespoon parmesan cheese
1 teaspoon finely chopped garlic
1 cup finely diced onion
3 tablespoons low-fat yoghurt
1 cup low-fat soymilk or low-fat milk

- Preheat oven to 180°C. Line a non-stick baking tray with paper.
- To make dahl, combine all ingredients except capsicum and carrot in a saucepan. Slowly bring to the boil and simmer for 1 hour, stirring frequently.
- Add capsicum and carrot and simmer for another 30 minutes or until dahl reaches desired consistency.
- While dahl is cooking, make damper by sifting flours and baking powder into a bowl. Add remaining ingredients and combine to form a sticky dough.
- Turn dough onto a lightly floured bench and knead. Shape into a long loaf shape and place on baking tray. With a sharp knife, make two shallow cuts across the top of loaf.
- Bake for 20–25 minutes or until crust is brown and loaf sounds hollow when tapped. Wrap in a tea towel and allow to cool slightly.

Serve dahl with warm slices of damper and a green salad (see pages 150–1). Also serve with a fresh carrot and capsicum juice.

Serves 6

Eggplant Dip

I can't imagine life without eggplants.

2 chargrilled young eggplants (see page 145), thinly sliced
1 x 300 g can chickpeas, well drained
½–⅔ cup freshly squeezed lemon juice
1–2 teaspoons crushed garlic
2 teaspoons cumin
freshly ground black pepper
pinch salt

- Combine all ingredients in a food processor and blend until nearly smooth. Allow to stand for at least 1 hour before serving for flavours to develop.

Serve generous amounts of dip on thick slices of Country Grain and Soy Bread (see page 73) or use as a filling for baked potatoes or baked sweet potatoes.

Eggplant and Pumpkin Asian Salad

Serves 6

In this recipe eggplant and pumpkin take on the fabulous flavours of Asia.

1 chargrilled young eggplant (see page 145), thinly sliced
500 g chargrilled pumpkin (see page 146), thinly sliced
200 g spinach, washed, chopped
100 g carrot, cut into thin julienne strips
100 g snow peas, cut into thin julienne strips
100 g red capsicum, seeded, cut into thin julienne strips
50 g bean shoots
¼ red onion, finely diced
¼ cup finely chopped fresh coriander

DRESSING
2 tablespoons lime or lemon juice
1 tablespoon balsamic vinegar
3 tablespoons low-salt soy sauce
2 tablespoons apple juice concentrate
1 tablespoon chilli sauce
½–1 teaspoon crushed garlic
1 teaspoon finely chopped fresh ginger

- Combine dressing ingredients in a glass jar and shake well.
- Combine all salad ingredients in a bowl and add dressing. Toss lightly, being careful not to break up the eggplant or pumpkin.

For variation add some cold cooked soya beans, chickpeas or cashew nuts to this salad when serving. Also serve with freshly squeezed orange juice or fresh carrot and capsicum juice.

Serves 4

Fasta Pasta Penne

You can make this pasta meal in minutes. It shows that fast food can be healthy and taste fabulous.

500 g penne
1 small onion, finely diced
1 teaspoon finely chopped garlic
¼ cup miso (see page 22)
600 g peeled pumpkin, cubed
100 g black olives
2 tablespoons low-salt soy sauce
500 g broccoli, thinly sliced
¼ cup pine nuts, dry roasted
¼ cup finely chopped basil

- Cook penne in a large pot of boiling water until soft, but still al dente. Drain, refresh under cold water and drain again well.
- In a heavy-based frying pan fat-free cook (see page 27) onion and garlic until soft and beginning to brown.
- Add miso, pumpkin and olives, cover and cook until pumpkin is soft.
- Add soy sauce and broccoli, cover and cook until broccoli is just tender and a vibrant green colour.
- Add pine nuts and basil.
- Add penne and toss to warm through.

Serve with a green salad (see pages 150–1) and plenty of crusty wholemeal bread.

Fresh Vietnamese Rolls

Serves 6–8

It's hard to imagine so much goodness in such a small parcel – and these rolls are completely fat-free. For that authentic Vietnamese flavour, it is worth seeking out a bunch of fresh Vietnamese mint.

100 g rice vermicelli noodles
200 g silken tofu, finely diced (see page 18)
2 carrots, grated
2 zucchini, finely diced
2 red capsicum, seeded, finely diced
1 Lebanese cucumber, peeled, seeded, finely diced
1 red onion, finely diced
leaves from 1 bunch Vietnamese mint, finely chopped

1 x 375 g packet Vietnamese rice paper wrappers (22 cm round)
500 g shredded lettuce

- Place noodles in a bowl and cover with boiling water. Stir for 3–5 minutes or until soft. Drain well and roughly chop.
- Combine noodles with tofu, all vegetables except lettuce and mint, and toss lightly.
- Place rice paper wrappers one at a time in a large dish of boiling water for 30–40 seconds or until softened. Carefully remove from water onto a clean, dry tea towel.
- Place some lettuce and filling mixture in the centre of a wrapper. Fold over one end and fold in the sides, then roll up with seam underneath. Repeat to make approximately 24 rolls.
- If you are not serving the rolls immediately, cover them with a damp cloth to keep them moist and fresh.

Serve with a selection of dipping sauces such as Sweet Chilli Dipping Sauce (see page 154), Spicy Oriental Dressing (see page 149), Tangy Tahini Dressing (see page 150) and low-salt soy sauce. Also serve with a fresh apple juice.

Serves 6

Fruit Scones

My mother made the best scones – these come a close second!

1½ cups unbleached white self-raising flour
½ cup wholemeal self-raising flour
1 cup chopped dried fruit (dates, apricots, sultanas, mixed peel)
2 tablespoons low-fat yoghurt or mashed silken tofu (see page 18)
1 tablespoon freshly squeezed lemon juice
¾ cup low-fat soymilk or low-fat milk
additional low-fat soymilk or low-fat milk

- Preheat oven to 210°C. Line a non-stick baking tray with paper.
- Sift flours into a bowl. Add dried fruit and coat well with flour.
- Combine yoghurt or tofu and lemon juice and gently mix into fruit mixture until it resembles breadcrumbs. Add enough milk to make a soft dough.
- Turn dough out onto a lightly floured bench and knead just a little. Divide into 6 even portions, and place close together on baking tray. Brush tops with a little extra milk.
- Bake for 15–20 minutes. Wrap scones in a tea towel to cool slightly.

Serve plain, or with low-fat cottage cheese or mashed silken tofu and sugar-free jams.

Minestrone Soup

Serves 6–8

Not just a soup, more like a meal in a bowl.

1–2 teaspoons crushed garlic
1 onion, chopped
2 large carrots, sliced
2 sticks celery, thinly sliced
1 large potato, peeled, cubed
20 French beans, topped, tailed and cut into 4
2 small zucchini, sliced
1 red capsicum, seeded, roughly chopped
1 x 425 g can salt-free tomatoes and juice
2 litres water or Vegetable Stock (see pages 156–7)
¼ cup salt-free tomato paste
1 teaspoon basil
½ teaspoon oregano
½ teaspoon marjoram
¼ teaspoon thyme
pinch of salt
freshly ground black pepper
1 cup cold, cooked leftover pasta (ribbons, macaroni, rigatoni, shells, spirals)
1 x 425 g can red kidney beans, well drained, rinsed
1 cup freshly chopped parsley

- Combine all ingredients except pasta, kidney beans and parsley in a large pot. Cover and slowly bring to the boil. Turn heat down and simmer for approximately 2½ hours.
- Add pasta and kidney beans and cook for a further 15 minutes, stirring every few minutes to prevent ingredients sticking to base of pot.
- Just before serving, add parsley.

Serve with plenty of crusty wholemeal bread and a green salad (see pages 150–1).

Serves 6

Panmolle with Beans

This is a variation of the traditional Tuscan summer salad dish of panmolle or panzanella, where a coarse-textured bread soaks up the flavours of good-quality Tuscan olive oil, balsamic vinegar, fresh tomatoes and basil.

1 loaf Country Grain and Soy Bread (see page 73) or other suitable bread
800 g ripe, firm tomatoes, peeled, seeded, roughly chopped
1 red onion, peeled, diced
1 cup fresh basil leaves
1 chargrilled red capsicum (see page 144), roughly chopped
1 chargrilled green capsicum, roughly chopped
1 tablespoon capers
100 g black olives, pitted, halved
1 x 300 g can butter beans, well drained
2 tablespoons balsamic vinegar
⅓ cup olive oil
freshly ground black pepper to taste

- Cut bread into 1–2 cm slices and toast both sides under a griller until just lightly browned. Cut each slice into 4 pieces.
- Combine remaining ingredients and toss well.
- Arrange a layer of bread in a salad bowl and add some salad. Add another layer of bread, then of salad and repeat until you have used all the ingredients. Save some salad mixture to garnish.
- If salad is too dry, drizzle a little more olive oil over before serving.

Serve with freshly squeezed orange juice or carrot and capsicum juice.

Pita Roll-ups

Pita bread rolled around your favourite filling is a perfect fast lunch meal. Made from just flour and water, the bread provides a fat-free base on which to build a variety of healthy, nutritious options. You'll want to eat these gourmet packages time and time again, so learn to improvise with leftover cooked vegetables, grilled tofu, cooked beans and lentils with tasty pasta sauces or dressings. To get you started, try these suggestions, representing the cuisines of Asia, Japan, Mexico and the Mediterranean. Always use fresh pita bread so it will roll around your filling choices easily without breaking. If your pita is more than a day old it can be revived and softened by microwaving for 10–20 seconds. If your fillings are very moist it is a good idea to seal the inside of the pita with a layer of spinach or lettuce or sheets of nori.

Pita – Asia

Serves 4

1 x 230 g packet rice noodles
200 g snow peas, trimmed
1 red capsicum, seeded, cut into thin strips
1 red onion, sliced
1 cucumber, cut into long thin slices
2 firm mangoes, peeled, cut into thin slices
½ cup torn fresh basil leaves
½ cup torn fresh mint leaves
¼ cup chopped dry roasted peanuts
1 tablespoon dry-roasted sesame seeds
½ cup Spicy Oriental Dressing (see page 149)
4 large pita breads
4–8 large lettuce leaves

- Place noodles in a bowl and cover with boiling water for a few minutes to soften. Separate noodles, drain and refresh under cold water. Drain well.
- Parcook snow peas and capsicum until they turn a vibrant colour. Refresh under cold water. Drain well.
- Combine all ingredients except pita bread and lettuce and toss well.
- Line each pita bread with 1–2 large lettuce leaves.
- Place an equal amount of filling down the centre of each pita. Fold one end up and over the filling and roll up, securing tightly.

Serve with freshly squeezed orange juice, fresh apple juice or fresh carrot and capsicum juice.

Serves 4–6

Pita – Japan

2 cups cold cooked rice (white or brown or a combination of both)
2 firm, ripe avocados, peeled, diced
1 cucumber, seeded, diced
1 teaspoon wasabi powder (see page 23)
1 teaspoon water
½ cup Creamy Mayonnaise (see page 148)
2 tablespoons chopped pickled ginger (see page 21)
4 large pita breads
4 nori sheets (see page 14)
1 bunch spinach, blanched, well drained
16 asparagus spears, blanched, well drained
100 g snowpea sprouts
4 spring onions, sliced diagonally

- Combine rice, avocado and cucumber in a bowl.
- Mix wasabi with water and add mayonnaise and pickled ginger. Gently mix through rice mixture.
- Place pita breads on a flat surface and line each one with a nori sheet and a layer of spinach.
- Place an equal amount of rice filling down the centre of each pita.
- Lay asparagus spears, snowpea sprouts and spring onions on top.
- Fold one end up and over the filling and roll up, securing tightly.

Serve with freshly squeezed orange juice, fresh apple juice or fresh carrot and capsicum juice.

Pita – Mediterranean

Serves 4

4 large pita breads
2 chargrilled young eggplants (see page 145) thinly sliced
2–4 tomatoes, sliced
8 cooked artichokes, well drained, halved
16–20 chargrilled mushrooms (see page 146)
100 g low-fat feta cheese, crumbled
10 olives, stoned, finely chopped
1 cup roughly chopped flat-leaf parsley

DRESSING
1 tablespoon olive oil
2 teaspoons balsamic vinegar
½–1 teaspoon crushed garlic
freshly ground black pepper

- Place pita breads on a flat surface and line with eggplant.
- Top with tomato, artichokes and mushrooms.
- Crumble an equal amount of feta cheese and chopped olives over each and add some parsley.
- Combine dressing ingredients in a jar and shake well. Spoon a little dressing over each pita.
- Fold one end up and over the filling and roll up, securing tightly.

Serve with freshly squeezed orange juice, fresh apple juice or fresh carrot and capsicum juice.

Serves 4

Pita – Mexico

2 cups red kidney beans
2 cups corn kernels
1 cup chopped green capsicum
1 cup chopped yellow capsicum
1 cup reduced-fat mozzarella cheese
4 large pita breads
400 g chopped lettuce

SALSA
1 chargrilled red capsicum (see page 144), finely chopped
2 firm Roma tomatoes, peeled, seeded, finely chopped
1 small Lebanese cucumber, seeded, finely chopped
½ red onion, finely chopped
½ cup finely chopped coriander
½ teaspoon cumin
1 teaspoon oregano
1 small red chilli, seeded, finely chopped
1 tablespoon balsamic vinegar
pinch of salt
1 cup low-fat firm yoghurt

- Combine beans, corn, capsicum and mozzarella in a bowl.
- Combine all salsa ingredients except for yoghurt and mix well.
- Place pita breads on a flat surface and line with some lettuce.
- Place an equal amount of bean filling down the centre of each pita and top with salsa and yoghurt.
- Fold one end up and over the filling and roll up, securing tightly.

Serve with freshly squeezed orange juice, fresh apple juice or fresh carrot and capsicum juice.

Potato Cakes with Capsicum and Cashew Salsa

Serves 4

Like me, I'm sure you'll find plenty of excuses to make this yummy salsa!

1 kg potatoes, peeled, chopped
1 onion, diced
2 tablespoons soy flour
2 egg whites
1 tablespoon finely chopped fresh basil
1 tablespoon finely chopped fresh mint
1 tablespoon finely chopped fresh coriander
2 teaspoons cumin
1–2 small red chillies, seeded, finely diced
pinch cayenne pepper

CAPSICUM and CASHEW SALSA
1 chargrilled red capsicum (see page 144), diced
1 firm, ripe avocado, peeled, stoned, diced
1 Granny Smith apple, cored, diced
½ cup chopped cashews
2 tablespoons finely chopped fresh coriander
juice of 1 lime or lemon
1 tablespoon balsamic vinegar
freshly ground black pepper

- Boil potatoes until tender. Drain, cool and roughly mash.
- Add onion, flour, egg whites, herbs and spices and mix well.
- Shape into round smooth cakes and refrigerate for at least 1 hour before cooking.
- Lightly oil a non-stick frying pan and heat.
- Cook potato cakes for 3 minutes on both sides until lightly brown. Keep warm.
- Make salsa by combining all ingredients and tossing well.

Serve warm potato cakes with a spoonful of Red Pepper Mayo (see page 149), some salsa and a green salad (see pages 150–1).

Opposite: Eggplant and Pumpkin Asian Salad (see page 76)

Potato Wedges with Creamy Sour Ricotta and Hot Guacamole

Serves 4–6

Potatoes are often thought of as a fattening food. Not necessarily true. It's all in the way you cook them and what you add to them. Here's a perfect example of how to cook and serve them while keeping saturated fat low.

4–6 large potatoes, washed, cut into thick wedges
1 tablespoon olive oil
1 tablespoon sesame seeds
1 teaspoon cumin
1 cup low-fat ricotta cheese
¼ cup low-fat milk or low-fat soymilk
juice of 1 small lemon

HOT GUACAMOLE
1 firm, ripe avocado, peeled, stoned, mashed
1 tomato, peeled, seeded, finely diced
1 small red onion, finely diced
1 small apple, peeled, diced
juice of a small lemon
1 small green chilli, seeded, finely chopped
1–2 teaspoons sweet chilli sauce (see page 19)

- Boil potato wedges until just tender. Drain well and allow to cool.
- Preheat oven to 220°C. Line a non-stick baking tray with paper.
- Combine potato wedges, oil, sesame seeds and cumin in a bowl, toss well and drain off any excess oil.
- Place on baking tray and bake until crisp and brown.
- While wedges are baking, blend ricotta and milk until smooth and creamy. Add just enough lemon juice to give mixture a slightly sour, tangy taste.
- To make guacamole, gently mix all ingredients together.

Serve wedges topped with sour cream and Hot Guacamole. A green salad (see pages 150–1) on the side makes this meal extra nutritious.

Opposite: Fresh Vietnamese Rolls (see page 78)

Pumpkin and Dill Scones with Three Bean Dip

Serves 4–6

Savoury scones such as these are ideal to serve with soup. Here, I've teamed them with a delicious spicy bean dip and some salad to make a meal of them. The canned beans which I've used are just as nutritious as the dried variety, but much easier to use.

1 cup unbleached white self-raising flour
1 cup wholemeal plain flour
2 tablespoons soy flour
2 teaspoons baking powder
2 tablespoons finely chopped fresh dill
1 cup firmly packed grated pumpkin
3 tablespoons low-fat yoghurt
1 cup low-fat soymilk or low-fat milk

THREE BEAN DIP

1 chargrilled red capsicum (see page 144), chopped
1 x 750 g can three bean mix, well drained
1 x 140 g salt-free tomato paste
½–1 teaspoon crushed garlic
2 teaspoons lemon juice
½ teaspoon cumin
½ teaspoon dry mustard
1 teaspoon basil
1–2 teaspoons sweet chilli sauce (see page 19)
1 small red onion, finely diced

- Preheat oven to 220°C. Line a non-stick baking tray with paper.
- Sift flours and baking powder into a bowl. Add dill and pumpkin and toss.
- Add yoghurt and milk and mix to a sticky dough consistency. Turn out onto a floured bench and knead lightly.
- Cut dough into shapes and place on baking tray.
- Bake for 12–15 minutes.
- Combine all dip ingredients except onion in a food processor and process until smooth. Fold through onion.

Serve scones hot from the oven with dip and a green salad (see pages 150–1).

Pumpkin, Coconut and Chickpea Soup

Serves 4–6

A perfect combination to warm you on a cold winter's day.

1 teaspoon sesame oil
1 teaspoon finely chopped fresh ginger
1 onion, diced
500 g peeled pumpkin, chopped
200 g potato, peeled, chopped
1 litre Vegetable Stock (see pages 156–7)
1 x 300 g can chickpeas, well drained
1 x 140 ml can low-fat coconut milk
2 tablespoons finely chopped fresh basil

- Place sesame oil, ginger and onion in a saucepan, cover and cook on low heat until onion is quite soft.
- Add pumpkin, potato and stock and cook until vegetables are soft.
- Using a hand-held blender, purée soup until smooth.
- Add chickpeas and purée until chickpeas are roughly chopped. Stir in coconut milk.
- Reheat, but do not boil. Add basil.

Serve immediately with thick slices of crusty wholemeal bread and a green salad (see pages 150–1) or with a slice of pizza (see pages 125–131).

Red Curry and Beans

Serves 4–6

Red curry paste, made from red chillies and spices, is hotter than green curry paste, which is made from the very mild green chilli and other spices. The coconut milk in this recipe, tones down the heat a little and the end result is warm, rather than hot.

2–3 tablespoons red curry paste (see page 20)
2 onions, sliced
2 young eggplants, cubed
250 g peeled pumpkin, cubed
1 x 300 g can chickpeas, well drained
1 x 400 ml can low-fat coconut milk
2 kaffir lime leaves, finely chopped (see page 21)
600 g green beans, topped and tailed, cut into 10 cm lengths
1 cup cous cous
1 cup boiling water
fresh coriander leaves for garnish
finely grated lemon rind for garnish

- Degorge eggplant if necessary (see pages 26–7).
- In a heavy-based frying pan, fat-free cook (see page 27) onion, eggplant, pumpkin and curry paste until vegetables are soft and beginning to brown.
- Add chickpeas, coconut milk, kaffir lime leaves and beans and bring to the boil. Reduce heat and simmer gently for 5 minutes.
- Place cous cous in a bowl and pour boiling water over. Stir, cover with plastic food wrap and stand until water is absorbed. Using a fork, toss cous cous to fluff lightly.
- Spoon curry over cous cous and garnish with fresh coriander and grated lemon rind.

Serve with wholemeal crusty bread. For a change you could serve this dish with cooked rice or any other suitable cooked grain. Also serve with a freshly squeezed orange juice or carrot and capsicum juice.

Serves 4–6

Red Lentil and Capsicum Soup

Thick, hearty and heavenly.

200 g red lentils, washed
2 red capsicums, seeded, chopped
2 onions, chopped
1 potato, peeled, chopped
1 teaspoon basil
1 teaspoon cumin
1 x 400 g can salt-free tomatoes in juice
1 litre Vegetable Stock (see pages 156–7)

- Combine all ingredients in a large saucepan and bring to the boil. Reduce heat and simmer until vegetables are soft.
- Purée until smooth.

Serve with thick slices of crusty wholemeal bread and a green salad (see pages 150–1). A slice of pizza (see pages 125–131) also goes well.

Roasted Red Capsicum Corn Cake with Red Pepper Mayo

Serves 10

Straight from the plains of Mexico.

- 2 x 310 g cans corn kernels, or 4–6 fresh corn cobs
- 1 cup unbleached white self-raising flour
- ½ cup unbleached wholemeal self-raising flour
- ½ cup coarse cornmeal (polenta)
- ⅛ teaspoon cayenne pepper
- 1 cup chopped spring onion
- 1 chargrilled red capsicum (see page 144), chopped
- 2 whole eggs
- 2 egg whites
- ¼ cup grapeseed or carotino oil
- 1 cup low-fat soymilk or low-fat milk
- 1 kg mixed salad greens, washed thoroughly

- Preheat oven to 180°C. Line a 6 cm deep non-stick 25 cm round springform tin with paper.
- If using fresh corn, remove husks and silky threads. Use a sharp knife to cut kernels from cob. If using canned corn, drain well and rinse under cold water to remove excess salt.
- Sift flours, cornmeal and pepper into a large mixing bowl. Add spring onion, corn and capsicum.
- In another bowl, combine eggs, egg whites, oil and milk and beat well. Add to corn mixture and combine well.
- Spoon mixture into tin and bake for 40–45 minutes.
- Cool slightly before removing from tin and slicing into wedges.

Serve warm with Red Pepper Mayo and a green salad (see pages 150–1) or with a favourite soup. This cake is delicious served cold and makes an ideal picnic food.

Serves 4–6

Soft Polenta with Ratatouille

This easy-to-prepare meal could only be described as homely.

1 tablespoon miso
½ cup boiling water
4½ cups water
2 cups cornmeal (polenta)
2 tablespoons grated parmesan cheese (optional)
freshly ground black pepper

1 quantity Ratatouille (see page 138)
1½ cups freshly chopped flat-leaf parsley

- Dissolve miso in boiling water. Place in a saucepan with water and bring to the boil.
- Slowly add cornmeal, stirring continuously, until mixture boils, thickens and begins to come away from the sides of the saucepan. Add cheese and pepper.
- Spoon Ratatouille over polenta and garnish with parsley.

Serve with crusty wholemeal bread and freshly squeezed orange juice.

Salad Sandwich

Serves 1

How do you make the perfect nutritionally balanced salad sandwich to eat at home, school, university or the office? First you begin with the perfect bread. It should be free of saturated fat, high in fibre or full of grains, preferably with some added soy or linseed. It should be low in salt and sugar and have no added colours or flavours. Next, you need a perfect low-fat, cholesterol-free spread. I love a little avocado mixed with Dijon mustard, but you can substitute tofu, low-fat ricotta or cottage cheese for the avocado and use other mustards or horseradish instead of the Dijon. And for the perfect filling – a variety of fresh ingredients.

2 slices bread (e.g. Country Grain and Soy Bread, page 73)
freshly ground black pepper
freshly chopped herbs (parsely, chives, mint, basil, coriander)

SANDWICH SPREADS
2 tablespoons avocado, mashed
1–2 teaspoons Dijon mustard
or
2 tablespoons mashed silken tofu (see page 18) or low-fat cottage cheese
½ teaspoon horseradish paste (available from supermarkets)
or
2 tablespoons mashed silken tofu or low-fat ricotta cheese
1 tablespoon finely chopped fresh chives
or
2 tablespoons mashed silken tofu or low-fat ricotta cheese

SANDWICH FILLINGS
Choose at least 6 of the following ingredients: mixed salad greens (butter lettuce, cos lettuce, radicchio, rocket or endive); spinach leaves; grated raw beetroot or cold cooked beetroot; snowpea sprouts or alfalfa sprouts; grated or sliced raw carrot or cold chargrilled carrot; red, yellow or green capsicum strips or cold chargrilled capsicum; cold cooked snowpeas; sliced tomato or sun-dried tomatoes; sliced or grated cucumber; sliced raw mushrooms or cold chargrilled mushrooms; grated raw zucchini or cold chargrilled zucchini; grated raw parsnip or cold chargrilled parsnip; cold chargrilled eggplant slices.

- Spread bread with your choice of spread.
- Top one slice of bread with your choice of fillings. Add pepper and herbs to taste. Top with the second slice of bread. Wrap well and refrigerate.

Serve sandwich with extra salad greens as a garnish. Also serve with freshly squeezed orange juice, fresh apple juice or fresh carrot and capsicum juice.

NOTE

To add more protein to a salad sandwich, add any of the following:

- mashed silken tofu
- grilled firm tofu slices
- mashed soya beans
- cooked egg whites
- Mixed Nuts and Seeds Butter (see page 153).

Spinach and Ricotta Cheese Pie

Serves 6

Although this version has much less saturated fat than the traditional recipe, it still contains a lot more fat than most of the recipes in this book. I suggest you keep it for a special occasion. For a delicious variation, substitute silken tofu for ricotta cheese.

800 g spinach, washed
500 g firm, low-fat ricotta cheese
150 g low-fat feta cheese
1 cup grated, reduced-fat mozzarella cheese
4 egg whites
1 cup chopped spring onions
1 teaspoon nutmeg
freshly ground black pepper
14 sheets filo pastry
1 tablespoon olive oil
¼ cup water
2 tablespoons sesame seeds

- Preheat oven to 200°C. Lightly oil a 20 cm springform tin.
- Blanch spinach until just wilted but still retaining its lovely green colour. Drain well and chop roughly.
- Combine spinach, cheeses, egg whites, spring onion, nutmeg and pepper and mix well.
- Combine olive oil and water and using a pastry brush, lightly wipe 8 sheets of filo pastry. Fold each sheet in half and lay them overlapping on the base and sides of the tin.
- Add spinach and cheese mixture.
- Wipe remaining sheets of filo pastry with combined oil and water and fold. Place on top of pie and press down the edges.
- Wipe a little combined oil and water over the top and sprinkle with sesame seeds.
- Bake for 40–45 minutes or until pie is lightly browned and firm in the centre.

Serve warm or cold with a green salad (see pages 150–1).

Spinach and Vegetable Roulade

Serves 4–6

Roulades are fun, easy to make and another great way to enjoy your daily dose of vegetables.

200 g spinach, washed
2 tablespoons unbleached white flour
1 tablespoon grated parmesan cheese
1 whole egg
5 egg whites
1 young chargrilled eggplant (see page 145), thinly sliced
2 chargrilled red capsicums (see page 144)

FILLING
200 g low-fat ricotta cheese or cottage cheese or silken tofu (see page 18)
2 tablespoons finely chopped chives
freshly ground black pepper

- Preheat oven to 180°C. Line a shallow slice tray with non-stick baking paper.
- Blanch spinach until just wilted but still retaining its fresh green colour. Drain well.
- Blend spinach, flour and parmesan in a food processor until smooth. Add whole egg and mix well. Pour mixture into a clean bowl.
- Beat egg whites until stiff peaks form. Gently fold into spinach mixture.
- Pour mixture into tray and spread evenly. Bake for 10–15 minutes or until firm.
- Remove roulade from oven and immediately up-turn onto a dry, clean tea towel. Carefully roll up and allow to cool.
- To make the filling, combine ricotta with chives and pepper and mix until smooth.
- To assemble, carefully unroll roulade. Arange a layer of chargrilled eggplant on top, followed by a layer of chargrilled capsicum. Spread filling along one end and roll up, with seam side down. Cover and refrigerate until firm before slicing.

Serve cold with a green salad (see pages 150–1) and crusty wholemeal bread.

Sunday Roast Vegetables with Pesto

Serves 4–6

With a few modifications, such as using healthy mono-unsaturated or polyunsaturated fat (vegetable oils) instead of unhealthy saturated fat (animal fats), you can achieve that truly authentic roast flavour. Choose a good-quality olive oil for marinating the vegetables.

2 potatoes, cubed (or use baby new potatoes)
1 sweet potato, cubed
2 parsnips, cubed
2 zucchini, cut into chunks
2 carrots, cut into chunks
8 baby onions
4–6 baby beetroot or 1 large beetroot cut into 4–6 pieces
500 g mixed salad greens
2 tablespoons balsamic vinegar
¼ cup Pesto (see page 152)

MARINADE
¼ cup olive oil
1 tablespoon grain mustard
pinch of salt (optional)
½ cup fresh rosemary sprigs

- Preheat oven to 220°C. Line a non-stick baking tray with paper.
- Combine oil, grain mustard, salt and rosemary. Marinate vegetables in this mixture for at least 1 hour prior to cooking, tossing often.
- Drain vegetables from marinade reserving rosemary. Place on baking tray and bake until well browned, crisp on the outside and soft on the inside.
- Toss salad greens with balsamic vinegar.

Serve vegetables on top of salad greens and spoon Pesto over. Also delicious served on cous cous (see page 6).

Tofu and Bok Choy Stirfry on Red Pesto Rice

Serves 4-6

The trick to a perfect stirfry is not to overcook the vegetables. The colours should always be vibrant and the vegetables should hold their firm shape.

2 teaspoons sesame oil
2 teaspoons olive oil
3 tablespoons low-salt soy sauce
2 tablespoons dry sherry
500 g firm tofu, sliced
¼ cup Red Pesto (see page 152)
1 cup rice (white or brown or a combination of both)
6 bok choy, washed, chopped
100 g snow peas, topped and tailed
2 carrots, cut into 6 cm lengths and thinly sliced lengthways

- Combine sesame oil, olive oil, soy sauce and sherry and marinate tofu for 30 minutes.
- Cook rice, drain and immediately stir through Red Pesto. Keep warm.
- Drain tofu, reserving marinade. Grill (see page 156) and keep warm.
- Heat marinade in a wok or frying pan and add vegetables. Stirfry until just cooked and vibrant in colour. Use a little extra soy sauce or vegetable stock if necessary.
- Add tofu and toss.

Serve with freshly squeezed orange juice or fresh carrot and capsicum juice.

Tomato and Olive Cake

Serves 12

A yummy savoury alternative to the lunch-time salad sandwich.

1½ cups unbleached white self-raising flour
½ cup unbleached wholemeal self-raising flour
½ cup grated parmesan cheese
½ cup sun-dried tomatoes, well drained, finely chopped
½ cup finely chopped olives
½ cup finely chopped spring onion
1 whole egg
3 egg whites
½ cup grapeseed oil
1 cup low-fat soymilk or low-fat milk
10 olives, pitted, halved
1 cup finely chopped fresh parsley

- Preheat oven to 180°C. Line a 6 cm deep 25 cm round springform tin with baking paper.
- Sift flours into a large mixing bowl. Add cheese, sun-dried tomatoes, chopped olives and spring onion.
- In another bowl, combine egg, egg whites, oil and milk and beat well. Add to tomato and olive mixture and mix well.
- Spoon mixture into prepared tin. Arrange olive halves on top.
- Bake for 40–45 minutes or until cake is firm in the centre.
- Scatter parsley over cake and allow to cool slightly before removing from tin and slicing.

Serve warm with slices of fresh tomato and a green salad (see pages 150–1) or as an accompaniment to soup. This cake is also delicious served cold and makes an ideal picnic food.

Vegetable Dumplings with Sweet Chilli Dipping Sauce

Serves 4-6

You'll want to make these tasty little dumplings time and time again. They are fast and filling.

1.5–2 litres vegetable stock or water
1½ cups unbleached white self-raising flour
1 cup grated or finely chopped mixed vegetables (zucchini, carrot, red capsicum)
2 spring onions, finely diced
¼ cup fresh or frozen peas
freshly ground black pepper
3 egg whites
½ cup low-fat soymilk or low-fat milk
½ cup Sweet Chilli Dipping Sauce (see page 154)

- Bring stock or water to the boil in a deep, wide saucepan. Reduce heat to a gentle simmer.
- Sift flour into a medium-sized bowl. Add vegetables, spring onion, peas and pepper.
- Mix egg whites and milk together and stir into vegetable mixture to make a sticky dough.
- Drop spoonfuls of mixture into simmering liquid, cover and cook for approximately 10 minutes. The dumplings will expand and float to the surface.

Serve with Sweet Chilli Dipping Sauce and a green salad (see pages 150–1).

Vermicelli Fruit Slaw

Serves 4–6

A light, refreshing lunch for the middle of summer.

100 g vermicelli rice noodles
1 red onion, sliced
1–2 apples, quartered, thinly sliced
1–2 pears, quartered, thinly sliced
2 green mangoes, peeled, stoned, thinly sliced
1 cup very thinly sliced cabbage
1 small Lebanese cucumber, seeded, sliced
2 spring onions, finely chopped
3 tablespoons chopped pickled ginger
½ cup chopped mint leaves
¼ cup chopped coriander leaves

DRESSING

¼ cup low-salt soy sauce
½–1 teaspoon crushed garlic
2 tablespoons rice wine vinegar (see page 25)
1 teaspoon sesame seeds
pinch of salt or cayenne pepper
2 teaspoons sesame oil
1 teaspoon finely grated lime or lemon rind

- Pour boiling water over noodles and stir until tender. Drain well and refresh under cold water. Drain again and roughly chop.
- Combine with all other salad ingredients in a large bowl.
- Combine dressing ingredients in a jar and shake well. Pour over salad and toss well.

Serve in bowls with chopsticks.

NOTE

To add more protein to Vermicelli Fruit Slaw add any of the following:

- grilled, firm tofu slices
- soya beans
- chickpeas
- cooked egg whites
- cashew nuts
- pumpkin seeds, sunflower seeds, sesame seeds

Zucchini Pancakes with Avocado and Apple Salsa

Serves 4-6

A fun, cheap way to eat the very versatile zucchini.

1 cup unbleached white self-raising flour
½ cup wholemeal plain flour
1 teaspoon baking powder
1 cup grated zucchini
1 tablespoon finely chopped fresh basil
1 tablespoon finely chopped fresh dill
1 tablespoon finely chopped fresh chives
2 tablespoons finely chopped onion
4 egg whites
1 teaspoon turmeric
1 cup low-fat soymilk or low-fat milk
fresh coriander leaves for garnish

AVOCADO and APPLE SALSA
1 avocado, peeled, diced
1 red-skinned apple, cored, diced
1 red onion, diced
200 g Lebanese cucumber, seeds removed, finely chopped
½ cup Creamy Mayonnaise (see page 148)
1 tablespoon lemon juice
freshly ground black pepper

- Sift flours and baking powder into a bowl and add zucchini, herbs and onion.
- Combine egg whites, turmeric and milk in a blender and blend until smooth. Add to zucchini mixture and mix together to make a smooth batter.
- Lightly oil a non-stick frying pan and place over heat. Drop in spoonfuls of batter. Cook for 2 minutes on each side until brown.
- To make salsa, combine all ingredients and toss well.

Top pancakes with salsa and garnish with coriander. Also serve with freshly squeezed orange juice or fresh carrot and capsicum juice.

Dinner Recipes

Dinner and lunch meals can be interchanged depending on your tastes and time constraints. I certainly have more time in the evening to linger over recipes that need a little more planning, preparation and cooking time.

Recipes such as chargrilled vegetable lasagne, baked lentil-filled eggplant, spinach and ricotta cannelloni, fried rice and homemade pizzas can be fun to make as well as fabulous to eat.

I particularly like this time when I can unhurriedly prepare the evening meal and unwind after a busy and fulfilling day. There's definitely something therapeutic in slowing down the pace and sipping a good red wine as one or two of the family gather to share the news of their day, while I prepare favourite vegetables, cook a rich flavoursome pasta sauce or stir a slow-cooking risotto.

Vegetable dinners are easily prepared and can satisfy the whole family. Make just one of these recipes for a simple, delicious meal or serve a smorgasbord to cater for everyone's tastes and nutritional needs. Often it's the combination of one or two recipes that increases their nutritional value.

Baked Beans

Serves 6

Beans are an excellent source of essential dietary fibre and protein. They are about 4 per cent unsaturated fat, the good fat that lowers cholesterol, and also come packed with the B vitamins, calcium, iron and zinc. Soya beans contain essential omega 3 fatty acids.

2 teaspoons olive oil
1 onion, finely diced
1 teaspoon crushed garlic
¼ teaspoon cumin
¼ teaspoon garam masala
¼ teaspoon coriander
2 teaspoons paprika
2 tablespoons low-salt soy sauce
1 red capsicum, seeded, cut into strips
2 zucchini, cut into rounds
1 x 800 g can salt-free tomatoes and juice, chopped
1 tablespoon tomato paste
2 x 300 g cans soya beans, well drained
1 cup roughly chopped fresh parsley or spring onions (green part mainly) for garnish

Variation
Instead of soya beans, use butter beans, red kidney beans or a combination of all three.

- Place the first 7 ingredients in a heavy-based frying pan and fat-free cook (see page 27) until onion is soft and beginning to brown.
- Add soy sauce and cook for another minute.
- Add capsicum, zucchini, tomatoes and juice and tomato paste, cover and cook slowly for 15–20 minutes.
- Add soya beans, cover and cook for a further 5–10 minutes.

Serve on thick slices of wholemeal toast and garnish with parsley or spring onions. This recipe also makes a delicious filling for baked potatoes, eggplants or capsicums.

Baked Eggplants with Cous Cous and Green Curry Vegetables

Serves 4–6

Cous cous and vegetables flavoured with a not-too-hot green curry paste make an ideal filling for baked eggplants. You could also try it in baked capsicums or baked baby pumpkins.

2–3 young eggplants
2 teaspoons olive oil
1 teaspoon crushed garlic
1 onion, diced
3 teaspoons green curry paste (see page 20)
400 g peeled pumpkin, roughly chopped
1 cup peas, fresh or frozen
2 cups cooked Cous Cous (see page 146)
¼ cup finely chopped fresh coriander
¼ cup finely chopped fresh basil

2 cups White Sauce (see page 155)
½ cup sesame seeds

- Preheat oven to 180°C.
- Cut eggplants in half, lengthways. Scoop out flesh, making a boat-like shape with sides approximately 1 cm thick all around. Roughly chop flesh. Degorge if necessary (see pages 26–7).
- In a heavy-based frying pan, place oil, garlic, onion, curry paste and eggplant flesh and cook until soft.
- Add pumpkin and peas, cover and continue cooking slowly until pumpkin is soft.
- Add cous cous, coriander and basil.
- Place eggplant shells, base side down, in a large, rectangular baking dish. Spoon equal amounts of filling into shells. Top with White Sauce and sesame seeds.
- Cover and bake for 45 minutes. Uncover and cook for a further 15 minutes.

Serve with a green salad (see pages 150–1).

Baked Eggplants with Red Lentils and Vegetables

Serves 4–6

So easy to prepare. In this recipe there are lots of different textures and colour-contrasting ingredients that create a flavoursome feast in minutes. Add a green salad with some ripe Roma tomatoes and you have a gourmet meal in no time at all.

2–3 young eggplants
1 cup red lentils
1 litre water
100 g leek, washed thoroughly, sliced
½–1 teaspoon crushed garlic
2 teaspoons red curry paste (see page 20)
200 g peeled pumpkin, finely chopped (or carrot or sweet potato)
100 g mushrooms, thinly sliced
1 zucchini, thinly sliced
2 cups White Sauce (see page 155)
1 cup breadcrumbs (or wheatgerm)
1 teaspoon poppy seeds
½ cup reduced-fat mozzarella

- Cut eggplants in half, lengthways. Scoop out flesh, making a boat-like shape with sides approximately 1 cm thick all round. Discard flesh and degorge if necessary (see pages 26–7).
- Cook lentils in water until soft, approximately 15–20 minutes. Drain well.
- Preheat oven to 180°C.
- In a heavy-based frying pan, fat-free cook (see page 27) leek, garlic, curry paste, pumpkin, mushroom and zucchini until soft and beginning to brown. Add lentils.
- Place eggplant shells, base side down, in a large, rectangular baking dish. Spoon equal amounts of filling into shells. Top with White Sauce.
- Combine breadcrumbs, poppyseeds and cheese and sprinkle over top of eggplants. Cover and bake for 45 minutes. Uncover and cook for a further 15 minutes or until tops are lightly browned.

Serve with a green salad (see pages 150–1).

Baked Semolina Gnocchi with Rich Tomato and Basil Sauce

Serves 6

This is my gnocchi-in-a-hurry recipe!

1 cup coarse semolina
1 litre water
½ cup grated parmesan cheese
½ cup chopped spring onion (green part only)
4 egg whites, lightly beaten
freshly ground black pepper

RICH TOMATO and BASIL SAUCE
1 onion, finely diced
1 cup dry white or red wine
1 x 800 g can salt-free tomatoes and juice
2–3 tablespoons salt-free tomato paste
1 tablespoon apple juice concentrate
½ teaspoon dried basil
½ cup freshly chopped basil
pinch of salt (optional)
freshly ground black pepper

- Preheat oven to 200°C. Lightly oil an 18 cm × 28 cm baking dish.
- Place semolina and water in a saucepan and cook over a low heat, stirring continuously, until mixture begins to boil and thicken. Continue cooking until mixture resembles thick porridge, but is not too dry.
- Remove from heat and stir in cheese and spring onion. Add egg whites and beat well, then add pepper.
- Turn mixture into baking dish and bake for 45 minutes or until gnocchi is firm and lightly browned on top. Cut into six equal portions and keep warm.
- While gnocchi is baking, place sauce ingredients, except the fresh basil, salt and pepper, in a saucepan and bring to the boil. Reduce heat and simmer for 20–30 minutes, stirring frequently, until sauce is a rich red colour and quite thick.
- Add fresh basil, salt and pepper to taste and cook for a few more minutes.

Serve gnocchi topped with sauce and garnished with extra fresh basil, accompanied by cooked snowpeas, spinach or asparagus spears. Also serve with fresh carrot and capsicum juice.

Bok Choy and Tofu Rolls with Tangy Tahini Dressing

Serves 4

Super-simple and simply scrumptious.

2 tablespoons olive oil
½–¾ cup water
1 x 375 g packet filo pastry
¼ cup sesame seeds (optional)
⅔ cup Tangy Tahini Dressing (see page 150)

FILLING
1 kg bok choy, cooked, well drained, roughly chopped
500 g tofu, sliced, grilled (see page 156)
2 chargrilled red capsicums (see page 144), cut into thin strips

- Preheat oven to 200°C. Lightly oil a baking tray, or line with paper.
- Combine oil and water and lay 3 sheets of filo pastry on a clean, dry bench. Brush a little combined oil and water over each sheet and fold in half.
- Place some bok choy, tofu and capsicum at one end of each sheet, fold over edges and roll up. Brush a little more combined oil and water over each roll and scatter some sesame seeds over. Place on baking tray. Repeat with remaining pastry and filling to make 8 rolls.
- Bake for 30–40 minutes or until crisp and brown on both sides. Turn rolls during cooking to crisp and brown evenly.

Serve immediately with Tangy Tahini Dressing and a green salad (see page 150–1). Also serve with freshly squeezed orange juice.

Cannelloni of Spinach and Ricotta with a Cheesy Polenta Crust

Serves 6

This is an old favourite with a new crunchy crust topping.

12 dry lasagne sheets
500 g spinach, washed
400 g low-fat ricotta cheese
½–1 teaspoon nutmeg
1 egg white
freshly ground black pepper
1 quantity Rich Tomato and Basil Sauce (see page 109)
½ cup reduced-fat grated mozzarella cheese
¼ cup grated parmesan cheese
¼ cup coarse cornmeal (polenta)

- Preheat oven to 180°C.
- Cook lasagne sheets 2–3 at a time in a large pot of boiling water until they are soft but still al dente. Lay on a dry tea towel to drain well.
- Steam cook (see page 29) spinach until just soft, refresh under cold water, drain well and roughly chop.
- Combine spinach, ricotta, nutmeg, egg white and pepper and beat well.
- Take a spoonful of spinach mixture and place along centre of a cooked lasagne sheet. Roll up to make a tube. Repeat with remaining lasagne sheets and filling.
- Spoon a little Rich Tomato and Basil Sauce over the base of a large, shallow, rectangular baking dish. Arrange filled cannelloni on top and cover with remaining sauce.
- Combine mozzarella, parmesan cheese and cornmeal and spoon over cannelloni.
- Cover and bake for 30–40 minutes.
- Uncover and cook for a further 10–15 minutes or until top is browned.

Serve with a green salad (see pages 150–1).

Corn and Potato Cakes on Spinach with Pumpkin Mash

Serves 4

Corn and cumin marry magnificently in these tasty little cakes, which come packed with fibre and flavour.

500 g potato, peeled, chopped
1 onion, diced
2 teaspoons cumin
2 teaspoons grapeseed or carotino oil
200 g cooked corn kernels
100 g carrot, sliced into thin rounds
2 egg whites or 1 whole egg
2 tablespoons finely chopped fresh parsley
2 extra egg whites
1 tablespoon water
1 cup wholemeal breadcrumbs
½ cup cornmeal (polenta)
additional grapeseed or carotino oil
600 g spinach

PUMPKIN MASH
600–800 g peeled pumpkin
freshly ground black pepper
2 tablespoons freshly chopped herbs (parsley, chives, thyme)

- To make mash, boil pumpkin until soft, drain well and mash. Add pepper and herbs. Keep warm.
- Boil potato until soft. Drain well and mash.
- Cook onion and cumin in oil over low heat until soft and fragrant. Add to potato with onion, corn, carrot, egg whites and parsley and stir well.
- Divide mixture into small, equal-size balls and flatten each one in the palm of your hand to form a cake. Place on a non-stick tray and refrigerate until firm.
- Combine extra egg whites and water. Beat lightly. Combine breadcrumbs and cornmeal. Dip cakes in egg white mixture and roll in breadcrumb mixture.
- Wipe a little extra oil over the base of a non-stick frying pan. Cook cakes until brown on both sides. Remove from pan and keep warm.
- Blanch spinach until just wilted. Drain well.

Serve cakes stacked on top of spinach with pumpkin mash on top.

Serves 4–6

Curried Greens on Two Rices

Perfect for a cold winter's night. The vegetables listed are only a suggestion, so chop and change them depending on what's in season. The combination of rices and chickpeas provides plenty of protein and lots of essential fibre.

1 teaspoon sesame oil
2 teaspoons finely chopped fresh ginger
½ teaspoon curry powder
½ teaspoon cumin
½ teaspoon coriander
½ teaspoon garam masala
1 tablespoon finely chopped lemon grass
1 onion, diced
1 bunch bok choy, washed, stems removed, chopped
100 g snow peas, topped, tailed
100 g broccoli, thinly sliced
100 g red capsicum, seeded, thinly sliced
200 g carrot, sliced into thin rounds
200 g mushrooms, sliced
2 cups vegetable stock
1 x 400 ml can low-fat coconut milk
1 tablespoon cornflour
¼ cup freshly chopped coriander
1 cup cooked brown rice
1½ cups cooked white rice
1 x 300 g can chickpeas, drained, roughly chopped

- Place first 8 ingredients in a heavy-based frying pan and fat-free cook (see page 27) until onion is soft and beginning to brown and spices are fragrant.
- Add bok choy, snow peas, broccoli, capsicum, carrot, mushrooms and stock, cover and cook slowly until vegetables are just soft and a vibrant colour.
- Mix a little coconut milk with cornflour to make a paste. Stir paste into remaining coconut milk and add to vegetables, stirring gently until mixture boils and thickens.
- Just before serving add coriander.
- Combine rices and chickpeas, cover with boiling water for a few minutes to warm through. Drain well.

Spoon vegetables and sauce over rice mixture. Serve with crusty wholemeal bread.

Fettuccine with Creamy Red Sauce and Olives

Serves 4

Pasta doesn't spread our waistlines or raise cholesterol levels, but traditional pasta sauces, made with full-fat cream and cheese, can. If you use low-fat ingredients and just a little cheese for taste, pasta is definitely a healthy meal option.

400 – 500 g dry or fresh fettuccine
20 olives, stoned, chopped
¼ cup finely chopped fresh basil

CREAMY RED SAUCE
1 small onion, finely diced
1 teaspoon finely chopped garlic
½ cup white wine or vegetable stock
2 bay leaves
3 cups low-fat soymilk or low-fat milk
¼ cup cornflour
2 tablespoons sun-dried tomatoes, well drained, puréed
2 chargrilled red capsicums, (see page 144), puréed
2 tablespoons grated parmesan cheese
6 Roma tomatoes, peeled, seeded, thinly sliced

- Cook fettuccine in a large pot of boiling water until soft but still al dente. (Fresh pasta will cook in half the time). Drain, refresh under cold water and drain again well.
- In a heavy-based frying pan, fat-free cook (see page 27) onion and garlic until soft and beginning to brown.
- Add wine or stock and cook for a further few minutes. Add bay leaves.
- Mix a little milk with cornflour to make a paste. Pour remaining milk into pan and slowly bring sauce to the boil. Add cornflour mixture, stirring continuously until sauce boils and thickens. Remove bay leaves.
- Stir in sun-dried tomato purée and red capsicum purée. Add parmesan cheese and tomatoes.
- Add drained pasta and toss well to coat evenly with sauce and warm through.
- Add olives and basil just before serving.

Serve with cooked snow peas or asparagus and a green salad (see pages 150–1). Also serve with plenty of crusty wholemeal bread.

Fried Rice with Oven-Baked Onions and Mushrooms

Serves 4-6

For good fried rice I like to drain al dente cooked rice, run it under cold water, drain it again, then wrap it in two or three tea towels and allow it to sit on the bench for a couple of hours to get all the moisture out of it.

4 egg whites
1 red onion, thinly sliced
200 g mushrooms, sliced
2 teaspoons dried basil
1 tablespoon olive oil
200 g red capsicum, seeded, chopped
200 g broccoli, sliced
1 cup frozen peas
2 tablespoons low-salt soy sauce
1 cup cold, cooked, well-drained brown rice
1 cup cold, cooked, well-drained white rice
1 cup spring onion, sliced diagonally
freshly ground black pepper
pinch of salt (optional)

- Preheat oven to 200°C. Lightly oil a non-stick frying pan and a shallow baking dish.
- Beat egg whites lightly and pour into frying pan. Cook on both sides until firm. Remove from pan and chop roughly.
- Place onion, mushrooms, basil and oil in baking dish. Bake until onions and mushrooms are soft and lightly browned.
- Place capsicum, broccoli, peas and soy sauce in another pan, cover and gently cook to soften vegetables.
- Add rice, baked onion and mushroom mixture and chopped egg whites and cook, tossing continuously, until rice is heated through.
- Add spring onion, pepper and salt.

Serve in individual bowls or wrap spoonfuls in large lettuce leaves. Also serve with fresh carrot and capsicum juice.

Honey and Soy Noodles with Vegetables

Serves 4–6

Chinese wok cooking is not only fast and easy, it provides possibly the most nutritious way to eat our vegetables – al dente and vibrant.

500 g hokkien noodles
2 teaspoons sesame oil
1 tablespoon finely chopped fresh ginger
2 tablespoons low-salt soy sauce
1 tablespoon honey
1 onion, sliced
2 carrots, cut into thin strips
1 red capsicum, seeded, cut into thin strips
1 yellow capsicum, seeded, cut into thin strips
200 g snow peas, topped and tailed, cut into thin strips
12 asparagus spears, diagonally sliced
100 g bok choy, chopped
1 small Lebanese cucumber, seeded, cut into thin strips
8 baby corn, halved
Vegetable Stock (see pages 156–7)
1 tablespoon cornflour
4 spring onions, diagonally sliced
2 teaspoons finely chopped fresh mint
2 teaspoons finely chopped fresh coriander

- Boil noodles until soft but still al dente. Refresh under cold water and drain well.
- Heat wok to hot and add sesame oil, ginger, soy sauce, honey, vegetables (except spring onions) and 1 cup stock. Cover and cook until vegetables are just soft and a vibrant colour.
- Mix cornflour and 2 tablespoons stock to make a paste. Stir into vegetables until sauce boils and thickens.
- Add noodles and toss to warm through.
- Add spring onions, mint and coriander.

Serve immediately with freshly squeezed orange juice or fresh carrot and capsicum juice.

Lasagne of Chargrilled Eggplants and Mushrooms

Serves 6–8

The endless combinations of colourful, chargrilled or steamed vegetables layered with lasagne sheets mean that you can eat lasagne night after night and never eat the same lasagne twice.

10 dry lasagne sheets
2 large chargrilled eggplants (see page 145), sliced
500 g chargrilled mushrooms (see page 146), chopped
½ cup cornflour
1 litre low-fat milk, low-fat soymilk or Vegetable Stock (see pages 156–7)
freshly ground black pepper
1 cup freshly chopped chives or chopped spring onion tops (green part only)
½ cup grated parmesan cheese

- Preheat oven to 180°C.
- Cook lasagne sheets 2–3 at a time in boiling water until soft but still al dente. Drain well and cool.
- Mix cornflour with a little milk or stock to make a paste.
- Heat chargrill pan to hot (but not too hot), add remaining milk and heat to nearly boiling. Add cornflour paste, stirring continuously until it boils and thickens.
- Add mushrooms, chives or spring onion and pepper.
- To assemble, place a layer of lasagne sheets on the base of a deep, rectangular lasagne dish and add alternative layers of eggplant, mushroom sauce and lasagne sheets. Finish with a layer of mushroom sauce.
- Sprinkle with parmesan cheese.
- Bake for approximately 40 minutes or until cheese has browned and sauce is bubbling.

Serve with a green salad (see pages 150–1).

Lasagne of Pumpkin and Coriander

Serves 4-6

In this not-so-typical lasagne recipe, the flavours of pumpkin and coriander blend together beautifully to produce a slightly Middle Eastern variation of the traditional Italian lasagne.

10 dry lasagne sheets
2 kg peeled pumpkin
2 teaspoons olive oil
2 large onions, diced
2 teaspoons crushed garlic
2 teaspoons cumin
1½ teaspoons dried coriander
2 whole eggs
2 egg whites
2 tablespoons grated parmesan cheese
½ cup finely chopped fresh coriander (parsley, basil or chives or a combination of these)
2 cups White Sauce (see page 155)
1 teaspoon grated parmesan cheese
½ cup pine nuts
¼ cup cashew nuts

- Preheat oven to 180°C.
- Cook lasagne sheets 2–3 at a time in boiling water until soft but still al dente. Drain well and cool.
- Boil pumpkin until soft. Drain well, mash and allow to cool.
- In a heavy-based frying pan, place oil, onion, garlic, cumin and coriander and cook until onion is soft and beginning to brown and spices are fragrant.
- When pumpkin is cold, add the cooked onion, eggs, egg whites, parmesan cheese and fresh coriander.
- Stir cheese into White Sauce.
- Place nuts in a food processor and blend until mixture resembles very fine breadcrumbs.
- To assemble, place a layer of lasagne sheets on the base of a deep, rectangular lasagne dish. Top with a third of the pumpkin filling and another layer of lasagne sheets. Repeat until you have 3 layers of pumpkin filling, finishing with a layer of lasagne sheets.
- Top with cheese sauce and sprinkle with nuts.
- Bake for approximately 45–55 minutes.

Serve with a green salad (see pages 150–1).

Lasagne of Spinach and Chargrilled Red Capsicums

Serves 6

Colourful and so delicious. Serve with a crisp green salad.

10 dry lasagne sheets
5–6 chargrilled red capsicums, (see page 144)
300 g spinach

TOMATO SAUCE
1 onion, diced
½–1 teaspoon crushed garlic
1 ½ cups dry white wine or vegetable stock or water
2 x 400 g cans salt-free tomatoes and juice
2 tablespoons salt-free tomato paste
½ teaspoon dried basil
½ teaspoon dried oregano
freshly ground black pepper

WHITE CHEESE SAUCE
1 cup White Sauce (see page 155)
1 tablespoon grated parmesan cheese

TOPPING
1 cup wholemeal breadcrumbs
1 tablespoon salt-free tomato paste
⅓ cup grated parmesan cheese

- Preheat oven to 180°C.
- Cook lasagne sheets 2–3 at a time in boiling water until soft but still al dente. Drain well and cool.
- Steam cook (see page 29) spinach and squeeze out moisture.
- To make tomato sauce, place all ingredients in a saucepan and cook slowly for 20–30 minutes or until sauce has reduced and thickened slightly.
- To make White Cheese Sauce, stir parmesan into White Sauce.
- Combine topping ingredients in a food processor and blend until mixture begins to stick together (don't overprocess).
- To assemble, place a layer of lasagne sheets on the base of a deep, rectangular lasagne dish. Top with a layer of capsicum, one-third of the Tomato Sauce and another layer of lasagne sheets. Add a layer of spinach, all the White Cheese Sauce and another layer of lasagne sheets. Add a layer of chargrilled capsicum, half the Tomato Sauce and another layer of lasagne sheets. Top with remaining chargrilled capsicum, and Tomato Sauce. Scatter topping over.
- Bake for 40–50 minutes until topping has browned and sauce is bubbling.

Linguine with Lentil Sauce

Serves 4–6

The protein in beans and lentils is not complete, therefore these foods are best combined with a protein complement such as grains or, in this case, pasta so they can deliver all nine amino acids the body needs for survival and function.

1 cup brown lentils
4 cups water
1 onion, sliced
2 teaspoons crushed garlic
1 cup grated carrot
1 small green capsicum, seeded, diced
1 x 425 g can salt-free tomatoes and juice
140 g salt-free tomato paste
1 cup Vegetable Stock (see pages 156–7) or white wine
2 teaspoons dried basil
½ teaspoon ground cumin
½ teaspoon dried coriander
500 g linguine
½ cup finely chopped fresh parsley

- Wash lentils thoroughly, cover with water and bring to the boil. Remove any foam that rises to the top and simmer for 25–30 minutes or until soft. Drain well.
- In a heavy-based frying pan, fat-free cook (see page 27) onion, garlic and carrot until soft and beginning to brown.
- Add all other ingredients except parsley and lentils and simmer for 15–20 minutes or until sauce begins to thicken.
- Add lentils and cook gently for a further 5–10 minutes. Add more stock if sauce thickens too quickly.
- Cook linguine in plenty of boiling water until al dente. Drain well.
- Toss with lentils, add parsley and serve immediately.

Serve with crusty wholemeal bread and a green salad (see pages 150–1).

Serves 4

Miso Soup

With some miso in the refrigerator and a packet of silken tofu in the pantry, you can always make a delicious, nutritious soup in absolutely no time at all. This is an excellent pick-me-up meal after a long day.

2 tablespoons miso paste (see page 22)
½ cup boiling water
5½ cups cold water
1 tablespoon salt-free tomato paste
2 zucchini, sliced into rounds
2 carrots, sliced into rounds
3 sticks celery, chopped
1 bunch asparagus spears, trimmed, cut into 4 cm pieces
1 teaspoon dried oregano
1 teaspoon dried basil
375 g silken tofu (see page 18), cubed
freshly ground black pepper
¼ cup freshly chopped flat-leaf parsley.

Variations

- Add finely chopped fresh ginger or garlic to the soup while it is cooking.
- Add shavings of parmesan cheese to individual servings.
- Add cooked soya beans, leftover pasta, chickpeas or lentils to the soup just before serving.

- Dissolve miso paste in boiling water.
- Place in a large saucepan with cold water, tomato paste, vegetables, oregano and basil and bring to the boil. Simmer until vegetables are just tender.
- Add tofu to warm through.
- Add pepper and parsley and serve immediately.

Serve with a green salad (see pages 150–1) and crusty wholemeal bread.

Moroccan Vegetable Casserole with Cous Cous

Serves 4–6

Ideally, keep this recipe for warming you up on a cold winter's evening. The slow cooking in the oven and the rich Moroccan spices flavour the very heart of the vegetables. It could also be served with rice and other cooked grains.

600 g pumpkin, peeled, cubed
200 g potatoes, peeled, cubed
200 g zucchini, cut into rounds
1 large onion, sliced
⅔ cup sultanas or raisins
⅓ cup freshly squeezed lemon juice
2 cups freshly squeezed orange juice
1–2 teaspoons paprika
1 teaspoon ground cumin
2 teaspoons finely chopped fresh ginger
2 teaspoons crushed garlic
1 cup cous cous
1 cup boiling water
½ cup finely chopped fresh coriander
1 teaspoon dried coriander
¼ cup finely chopped fresh mint
½ cup dry roasted cashews (optional)

- Preheat oven to 220°C.
- Place all ingredients except cous cous, boiling water, fresh and dried coriander, mint and cashews in a large casserole. Cover and cook slowly for 1½ hours or until vegetables are soft and liquid has reduced and thickened slightly.
- Place cous cous in a bowl. Add boiling water and stir. Cover with plastic wrap and allow to stand for 5 minutes. Remove plastic wrap and, using a fork, lightly fluff.
- Add fresh and dried coriander, mint and cashews to vegetables.
- Place cous cous on a serving dish and arrange vegetables on top.

Serve with low-fat yoghurt and crisp, thin, julienne slices of apple or pear.

Serves 6

Mushroom Pie

Mushrooms are an excellent source of B-group vitamins. They also contain the antioxidant mineral, selenium. This pie is delicious served with a crisp green salad (see pages 150–1).

200 g spinach, washed
200 g leeks, washed
½ cup white wine
1 teaspoon oregano
1 teaspoon basil
1 cup Vegetable Stock (see pages 156–7)
1 tablespoon cornflour
800 g chargrilled mushrooms (see page 146), roughly chopped
freshly ground black pepper

PASTRY
4 cups wholemeal breadcrumbs
¾ cup parmesan cheese
½ cup freshly chopped parsley
3 tablespoons tomato paste

- Preheat oven to 180°C. Lightly oil a shallow 20 cm pie dish.
- Place breadcrumbs on a non-stick baking tray in the oven to dry out a little. Allow to cool.
- Combine pastry ingredients in a food processor and blend until mixture begins to stick together. Do not over-process.
- Press half of pastry over the base and sides of pie dish. Bake for 10–15 minutes or until brown and slightly crisp.
- Cook leeks until soft and beginning to brown. Add spinach and allow to wilt slightly. Add wine and herbs and cook for a minute. Add stock, reserving a little.
- Mix reserved stock with cornflour to make a paste. Stir spinach into mixture and cook until mixture boils and thickens. Add mushrooms and pepper to taste. Allow to cool.
- Spoon filling into cooked pastry case. Top with remaining pastry and spread to cover pie. Bake for 40 minutes.
- Allow to cool a little before cutting into slices and serving.

Pasta and Vegetable Terrine

Serves 4-6

The presentation of this colourful terrine is all-important. Individual slices look sensational served on large white plates, garnished simply with a few salad greens, halved cherry tomatoes and black olives.

8 dry lasagne sheets
200 g carrots, cut into long, thin slices
200 g zucchini, cut into long, thin slices
2 large chargrilled eggplants, (see page 145)
2 large chargrilled red capsicums, (see page 144)
½ cup Pesto (see page 152)
balsamic vinegar

- Cook lasagne sheets 2–3 at a time in a large pot of boiling water until soft. Drain well on a tea towel and cool.
- Boil carrot and zucchini until soft and drain well.
- To assemble, cover the base of a deep 10 cm × 20 cm rectangular terrine dish with a layer of lasagne sheets. Spread with a little of the Pesto. Build layers of vegetables, lasagne sheets and Pesto, finishing with a layer of lasagne sheets.
- Pour over a little balsamic vinegar, cover and place a weight on top. Refrigerate for at least 2 hours before unmoulding onto a platter and slicing.

Serve with a green salad (see pages 150–1). You could also serve this terrine with leftover butter beans, chickpeas, red kidney beans or soya beans flavoured with a little Balsamic Vinaigrette (see page 147).

Makes 1 large pizza base

Pizza Dough

Pizza makes an ideal, no-fuss, healthy vegetarian meal. Once you master the basics of making Pizza Dough and Pizza Sauce, you can make your own gourmet combinations using any topping ingredients you particularly like. When cooked, this wholemeal pizza crust is crunchy on the outside and deliciously soft on the inside.

7 g sachet dry yeast
1 cup unbleached white plain flour
1 cup unbleached wholemeal plain flour
1 teaspoon apple juice concentrate
1 cup lukewarm water

- Combine yeast and flours in a medium-sized bowl, and make a small well in the centre. Add apple juice concentrate and water.
- Mix to a soft dough consistency and roll out onto a lightly floured bench top.
- Knead dough by hand for approximately 5 minutes or until it is smooth and elastic. Place in a lightly oiled bowl and cover. Allow to stand for approximately 30 minutes or until dough has doubled in size.
- Knock dough back to its original size, knead a little more and, if using immediately, roll out to fit a lightly oiled, 30 cm pizza tray. If not using immediately, roll into a ball, cover with plastic wrap and refrigerate. The cold air will slow down the rising process. Allow the dough to come to room temperature before rolling it out.

Pizza Sauce

Serves 2–4

There are two pizza sauces to try. One you can do in a matter of seconds and the other needs to be cooked but is possibly more flavoursome.

UNCOOKED PIZZA SAUCE

1 x 400 g can salt-free tomatoes and juice
2 tablespoons salt-free tomato paste
½–1 teaspoon crushed garlic
handful of fresh basil leaves
freshly ground black pepper

- Place all ingredients in a blender and blend until smooth.
- Refrigerate any leftover sauce.

COOKED PIZZA SAUCE

1 onion, finely diced
½–1 teaspoon crushed garlic
1 x 400 g can salt-free tomatoes and juice, puréed
2 tablespoons salt-free tomato paste
1 teaspoon dried basil
½ teaspoon dried oregano
½ cup white wine or Vegetable Stock (see pages 156–7)
½ cup water
freshly ground black pepper

- Place all ingredients in a small saucepan and cook for 15–20 minutes or until sauce has reduced and thickened. Cool before using.
- Refrigerate any leftover sauce.

Serves 2–4

Margherita Pizza

1 quantity Pizza Dough (see page 125)
1 large red onion, cut into wedges
2 teaspoons olive oil
1 cup Pizza Sauce (see page 126)
¾ cup grated reduced-fat mozzarella cheese
6–8 Roma tomatoes, halved
¼ cup fresh basil leaves
freshly ground black pepper

- Preheat oven to 220°C–250°C. Lightly oil a 30 cm pizza tray. Roll out Pizza Dough to fit tray.
- Place onion on a small baking tray, drizzle with a little olive oil and place in hot oven or under a griller for 10–15 minutes or until soft and browned.
- Spread pizza base with Pizza Sauce and add cheese.
- Arrange tomato and roasted onion evenly over pizza. Add basil and pepper. Bake for 10–15 minutes. Remove from oven, slice into 8 portions and serve immediately.

Serve with a green salad (see pages 150–1). Also serve with freshly squeezed orange juice or fresh carrot and capsicum juice.

Mediterranean Pizza

Serves 2–4

1 quantity Pizza Dough (see page 125)
1 cup Pizza Sauce (see page 126)
½ cup grated reduced-fat mozzarella cheese
2 chargrilled red capsicums (see page 144) cut into thin strips
100 g cherry tomatoes, halved
100 g yellow pear tomatoes, halved
½ cup pitted olives, chopped
100 g low-fat feta cheese, crumbled
¼ cup fresh basil leaves, finely shredded
freshly ground black pepper

- Preheat oven to 220°C–250°C. Lightly oil a 30 cm round pizza tray. Roll out Pizza Dough to fit tray.
- Spread pizza base with Pizza Sauce and add mozzarella cheese.
- Top base with capsicum, tomato and olives. Add feta cheese, basil and pepper.
- Bake for 10–15 minutes. Remove from oven, slice into 8 portions and serve immediately.

Serve with a green salad (see pages 150–1). Also serve with freshly squeezed orange juice or fresh carrot and capsicum juice.

Mexican Pizza

Serves 2–4

1 quantity Pizza Dough (see page 125)
1 cup Pizza Sauce (see page 126)
1 red onion, thinly sliced
1 small red chilli, seeded, finely diced
1 green capsicum, seeded, cubed
1 yellow capsicum, seeded, cubed
1 avocado, peeled, stoned, sliced
1 x 300 g can red kidney beans, well drained
¾ cup grated reduced-fat mozzarella cheese
1 tablespoon freshly chopped oregano or 1 teaspoon dried oregano

- Preheat oven to 220°C–250°C. Lightly oil a 30 cm round pizza tray. Roll out Pizza Dough to fit tray.
- Add onion and chilli to Pizza Sauce and spread pizza base with sauce.
- Top with capsicum, avocado and beans. Sprinkle cheese over and top with oregano.
- Bake for 10–15 minutes. Remove from oven, slice into 8 portions and serve immediately.

Serve with a green salad (see pages 150–1). Also serve with freshly squeezed orange juice or fresh carrot and capsicum juice.

Sweet and Sour Pizza

Serves 2–4

1 quantity Pizza Dough (see page 125)
¾ cup grated reduced-fat mozzarella cheese
1 chargrilled zucchini (see page 146), sliced thinly lengthways
1 chargrilled red capsicum (see page 144), roughly chopped
1 chargrilled yellow capsicum (see page 144), roughly chopped
2 cups peeled, chopped fresh pineapple or well drained, unsweetened canned pineapple
freshly ground black pepper
1 tablespoon sesame seeds
1 cup diagonally sliced spring onion

SWEET and SOUR SAUCE
2 teaspoons sesame oil
2 teaspoons fresh ginger
1 teaspoon crushed garlic
¾ cup pineapple juice
½ cup freshly squeezed orange juice
2 tablespoons apple juice concentrate
¼ cup low-salt soy sauce
1 tablespoon cornflour
1 tablespoon water

- Preheat oven to 220°C–250°C. Lightly oil a 30 cm round pizza tray. Roll out Pizza Dough to fit tray.
- To make the sauce, combine all ingredients except cornflour and water and bring to the boil. Simmer for 10 minutes.
- Combine cornflour and water to make a paste. Add to sauce, stirring continuously until sauce boils and thickens. Cool.
- Spread pizza base with Sweet and Sour Sauce and add cheese.
- Top with zucchini, capsicum and pineapple. Add pepper and sesame seeds.
- Bake for 10–15 minutes. Remove from oven and add spring onion. Slice into 8 portions and serve immediately.

Serve with a green salad (see pages 150–1). Also serve with freshly squeezed orange juice or fresh carrot and capsicum juice.

Vegetable Supremo Pizza

Serves 2–4

1 quantity Pizza Dough (see page 125)
1 cup Pizza Sauce (see page 126)
1 chargrilled eggplant, thinly sliced (see page 145)
1 small sweet potato, thinly sliced into rounds, steam cooked
1 chargrilled red capsicum (see page 144), cut into strips
200 g broccoli, cut into florets, steam cooked
¾ cup grated reduced-fat mozzarella cheese
16 thin asparagus spears, steam cooked
1 small red onion, sliced into rounds
freshly ground black pepper

- Preheat oven to 220°C–250°C. Lightly oil a 30 cm round pizza tray. Roll out Pizza Dough to fit tray.
- Spread pizza base with Pizza Sauce.
- Top with eggplant, sweet potato, capsicum and broccoli. Sprinkle cheese over.
- Bake for 10–15 minutes. Remove from oven and top with asparagus, onion and pepper. Slice into 8 portions and serve immediately.

Serve with a green salad (see page 150–1). Also serve with freshly squeezed orange juice or fresh carrot and capsicum juice.

Potato Gnocchi with Sweet Chilli Tomato Sauce

Serves 4–6

Gnocchi has a way of turning the humble potato into something special. You can make it ahead of time and refrigerate until needed.

1 kg potatoes, peeled
1 cup unbleached white plain flour
1 whole egg
3 egg whites
2 tablespoons grated parmesan cheese
1 cup finely chopped spring onions (green part mainly)
extra unbleached white plain flour
¼–½ cup grated parmesan cheese

SWEET CHILLI TOMATO SAUCE
3 x 425 g cans salt-free tomatoes and juice, puréed
1–2 tablespoons apple juice concentrate
1–2 teaspoons sweet chilli sauce (see page 19)
2 tablespoons salt-free tomato paste
1 carrot, grated
½ cup freshly chopped basil
pinch of salt (optional)

- Preheat oven to 200°C.
- Boil potatoes until soft, drain well, mash and allow to get cold.
- Add sifted flour to potato and beat well. Add whole egg, egg whites, parmesan cheese and spring onion and mix to a firm dough.
- Form into 18 balls and roll in extra flour. Using the back of a fork, press down on each gnocchi ball. Shake off excess flour.
- Place all sauce ingredients in a frying pan and bring to the boil. Turn heat down and simmer until carrot is soft. Pour sauce into a large 5 cm deep 30 cm × 20 cm rectangular baking dish.
- Place gnocchi balls in the sauce, preferably not touching each other.
- Scatter parmesan cheese over the top, cover and bake for 50–60 minutes. Uncover for the last 10 minutes of cooking time.

Serve with a green salad (see pages 150–1) and chargrilled mushrooms (see page 146).

Pumpkin Gnocchi with Mushroom and Leek Sauce

Serves 4–6

Another exciting, effortless way to enjoy pumpkin.

1 kg peeled pumpkin
1½ cups unbleached white plain flour
4 egg whites
pinch of cayenne pepper

MUSHROOM and LEEK SAUCE
800 g mushrooms, sliced
1 leek, washed, sliced
¼ cup white wine
¼–1 teaspoon dried dill
2 cups low-fat milk or low-fat soymilk or Vegetable Stock (see pages 156–7)
2 tablespoons cornflour
2 tablespoons finely chopped fresh parsley

- Preheat oven to 200°C. Lightly oil a non-stick rectangular baking dish or line with baking paper.
- Boil pumpkin until soft, drain well, purée and allow to go cold.
- Add sifted flour to pumpkin and beat well. Add egg whites and pepper and mix to a sticky dough consistency. Spoon into baking dish.
- Bake for 35–40 minutes or until firm and lightly browned on top. Remove from oven and cut into 12 equal portions.
- While gnocchi is cooking, make the sauce. In a heavy-based frying pan, fat-free cook (see page 27) mushroom and leek until soft and beginning to brown. Add wine and dill and cook slowly for 2–3 minutes.
- Combine a little milk with cornflour to make a paste.
- Add remaining milk to mushroom and leek and bring to nearly boiling. Add cornflour mixture and stir continuously until sauce boils and thickens. Add parsley.

Serve immediately with a green salad (see pages 150–1) or cooked spinach and chargrilled red capsicums (see page 144).

Pumpkin and Pine nut Macaroni Cheese

Serves 4–6

Everyone has a favourite macaroni cheese recipe. This one is low on the cheese and big on the macaroni, with some unexpected ingredients that take it from being a basic dish into the gourmet category.

- 300 g macaroni
- 1 litre White Sauce (see page 155)
- 2 tablespoons grated parmesan cheese
- ⅛–¼ teaspoon cayenne pepper
- 500 g peeled pumpkin, cooked, puréed
- 2–3 cups wholemeal breadcrumbs
- ¼ cup grated reduced-fat mozzarella cheese
- 1 tablespoon salt-free tomato paste
- ¼ cup pine nuts

- Preheat oven to 180°C. Lightly oil a baking dish.
- Cook macaroni in boiling water until al dente. Drain well and refresh under cold water.
- Combine White Sauce, parmesan cheese and cayenne pepper. Stir in pumpkin while it is still hot.
- Stir in macaroni. Spoon into baking dish.
- Combine breadcrumbs, mozzarella cheese and tomato paste in a food processor until mixture begins to stick together. Do not overprocess. Sprinkle over macaroni. Sprinkle pine nuts over the top.
- Bake for approximately 35–40 minutes.

Serve with a green salad (see pages 150–1), cooked spinach and crusty wholemeal bread.

Pumpkin and Ricotta Cannelloni with Leek and Mushroom Sauce

Serves 6

A delicious combination of soft, creamy ingredients wrapped up in a pasta parcel and covered in a scrumptious, not-too-heavy wine, leek and mushroom sauce. For extra goodness, serve with a fresh green salad (see pages 150–1).

12 dry lasagne sheets
500 g pumpkin, cooked, mashed, cold
500 g low-fat ricotta cheese
100 g chopped sun-dried tomatoes
100 g chopped black olives
1 egg white
½ cup finely chopped fresh parsley
2 tablespoons grated parmesan cheese

LEEK and MUSHROOM SAUCE
1 leek, washed, chopped
400 g mushrooms, chopped
1½ cups white wine
1½ cups Vegetable Stock (see pages 156–7)
1 tablespoon cornflour
freshly ground black pepper

- Preheat oven to 180°C.
- Cook lasagne sheets 2–3 at a time, in a large pot of boiling water until soft but still al dente. Drain well.
- Combine pumpkin, ricotta, sun-dried tomatoes, olives and egg white. Beat well.
- Place a spoonful of this mixture down the centre of a cooked lasagne sheet. Roll up to make a tube. Repeat with remaining lasagne sheets and filling.
- In a heavy-based frying pan, fat-free cook (see page 27) leek and mushroom until soft and beginning to brown. Add wine and cook for a few more minutes.
- Combine a little stock with cornflour to make a paste.
- Add remaining stock and pepper to sauce and bring to the boil. Add cornflour mixture, stirring continuously until sauce boils and thickens. Remove from heat.
- Spoon a little sauce over the base of a 5 cm deep 30 cm × 20 cm baking dish. Lay the cannelloni on top and spoon over remaining sauce. Cover and bake for 30–40 minutes.
- Remove cover and sprinkle on the combined parsley and parmesan cheese. Return to the oven and bake for 5–10 minutes.

Red Pepper Risotto

Serves 4-6

Traditionally risotto has a lot of butter and cheese to give it a unique creamy texture as well as taste. I think it's just as delicious with a hint of cheese. The creamy texture is really achieved in the way you energetically stir the rice while it is cooking.

1 leek, washed, chopped
2 teaspoons crushed garlic
1 teaspoon sweet chilli sauce (see page 19) or finely chopped fresh red chilli
2 cups arborio rice
½ cup white wine
1 litre hot Vegetable Stock (see pages 156–7)
2 chargrilled red capsicums (see page 144), puréed
1 tablespoon grated parmesan cheese (optional)

- In a heavy-based frying pan, fat-free cook (see page 27) leek, garlic and chilli until soft and beginning to brown.
- Add rice and wine, stir and cook for 1 minute.
- Add stock and stir well. Cover, reduce heat and cook slowly until all liquid is absorbed and rice is tender and creamy. Lift the lid every few minutes and give rice a good stir. This helps release the starchy coating on rice to give the dish its typical creamy (rather than gluggy) texture.
- Stir in capsicum and cheese.

Serve immediately with crusty wholemeal bread, cooked spinach or chargrilled eggplant (see page 145). Also serve with freshly squeezed orange juice or carrot and capsicum juice.

Serves 4-6

Risotto of Pumpkin and Peas

Choose a vibrant orange, fleshy rather than woody, pumpkin for this recipe. The cooked pumpkin will add colour as well as enhancing the creamy nature of the risotto in the final stages of stirring. Cold leftover risotto also makes delicious rice cakes.

2 onions, diced
1 teaspoon crushed garlic
2 teaspoons dried basil
1 tablespoon red curry paste (see page 20)
600 g pumpkin, peeled, cubed
2 cups arborio rice
½ cup white wine
1 litre hot Vegetable Stock (see pages 156–7)
1 cup fresh or frozen peas
1 tablespoon grated parmesan cheese (optional)

- In a heavy-based frying pan, fat-free cook (see page 27) onion, garlic, basil, red curry paste and pumpkin until soft and beginning to brown.
- Add rice and wine, stir and cook for 1 minute.
- Add stock and stir well. Cover, reduce heat and cook slowly, stirring well every few minutes, until all liquid is absorbed, pumpkin is soft and rice is tender and creamy.
- Add peas, cover and continue cooking until peas are soft.
- Stir cheese through.

Serve immediately with crusty wholemeal bread, cooked spinach and grilled tomatoes. Also serve with freshly squeezed orange juice or carrot and capsicum juice.

Risotto Ratatouille

Serves 4-6

Ratatouille is best described as a thick, full-of-flavour vegetable stew. It is delicious hot or can be served cold as a vegetable chutney. I like to make it at least a day in advance so the flavours are rich and wonderful.

1 young eggplant, cubed
2 onions, chopped
2 teaspoons crushed garlic
1 red capsicum, seeded, roughly chopped
1 zucchini, roughly chopped
400 g small mushrooms
1 x 425 g can salt-free tomatoes and juice
2 teaspoons basil
1 teaspoon oregano
ground black pepper
1 tablespoon salt-free tomato paste
½ cup red or white wine or Vegetable Stock (see pages 156–7)
2 tablespoons finely chopped fresh parsley

RISOTTO
1 onion, diced
1 teaspoon crushed garlic
2 cups arborio rice
½ cup white wine
1 litre hot Vegetable Stock (see pages 156–7)
1 tablespoon parmesan cheese (optional)

- Degorge eggplant if necessary (see pages 26–7).
- In a heavy-based frying pan, fat-free cook (see page 27) onion and garlic until soft and beginning to brown. Add remaining ingredients and bring to the boil. Reduce heat, cover and cook slowly for 30 minutes. Uncover and continue cooking for another 15–20 minutes or until sauce reduces and thickens.
- To make the risotto, fat-free cook onion and garlic in a heavy-based frying pan until onion is soft and beginning to brown.
- Add rice and wine, stir and cook for 1 minute.
- Add stock and stir well. Cover, turn heat down and cook slowly, stirring well every few minutes until all liquid is absorbed. The rice should be tender and creamy in texture, not gluggy.
- Add cheese and stir through.

To serve make a small well in the centre of the rice and add a large spoonful of the ratatouille. Also serve with freshly squeezed orange juice or carrot and capsicum juice.

Serves 8–10

Shepherd's Pie

My version of an old favourite. You can always halve the quantities if you don't have lots of mouths to feed, but this pie does keep well in the refrigerator and you can reheat individual serves in the microwave.

1.25 kg mixed chopped vegetables (zucchini, carrots, capsicums, broccoli, green beans, pumpkin, sweet potato)
2 chargrilled eggplants, thinly sliced (see page 145)

TOPPING
10 slices wholemeal or grain bread, crumbed
1 x 140 g tub salt-free tomato paste
½ cup grated parmesan cheese
1 cup fresh chopped parsley

GRAVY
1 litre Vegetable Stock (see pages 156–7)
2 teaspoons basil
freshly ground black pepper
¼ cup water
½ cup cornflour

- Preheat oven to 200°C.
- To make the topping, place all ingredients in a food processor and combine until mixture begins to stick together.
- Steam cook (see page 29) mixed vegetables until just soft.
- To make the gravy, bring stock to the boil and add basil and pepper. Combine water and cornflour to make a paste and stir this into the boiling stock, stirring continuously until mixture thickens slightly.
- Place all vegetables including eggplant in a large casserole, pour over gravy and cover with topping. Cover and bake for 40 minutes. Uncover and cook for a further 10–15 minutes to brown.

Serve with a green salad (see pages 150–1).

Spaghetti with Eggplant Sauce

Serves 4-6

Enjoy a little bit of Italy without ever needing to leave home.

500 g spaghetti
2 young eggplants, cubed
2 onions, diced
2 teaspoons crushed garlic
1 x 800 g can salt-free tomatoes and juice
½ cup red wine
2 tablespoons capers
freshly ground black pepper
¼ cup finely chopped fresh basil

- Cook spaghetti in boiling water until al dente. Drain well and keep warm.
- Degorge eggplants if necessary (see pages 26–7).
- In a heavy-based frying pan, fat-free cook (see page 27) onion, garlic and eggplant until soft and beginning to brown.
- Add tomatoes and their juice and red wine, cover and cook slowly for 20–30 minutes.
- Just prior to serving, add capers, pepper and basil.

Serve with a green salad (see pages 150–1) and plenty of crusty wholemeal bread. Also serve freshly squeezed orange juice.

Spring Rolls with Sweet Chilli Dipping Sauce

Serves 4-6

A little fiddly but worth the trouble.

2 tablespoons olive oil
½–¾ cup water
1 x 375 g packet filo pastry

FILLING
500 g peeled potato, grated
500 g peeled pumpkin, grated
500 g spinach, cooked, well drained, roughly chopped
1 zucchini, grated
1 red capsicum, seeded, finely chopped
½ cup chopped spring onion
2 teaspoons finely chopped fresh ginger
1–2 teaspoons sweet chilli sauce (see page 19)
1 tablespoon finely chopped fresh basil
1 tablespoon finely chopped fresh coriander or mint

- Preheat oven to 200°C. Lightly oil a baking tray or line with paper.
- Place potato in a colander and run under cold water to remove starch. Combine potato and pumpkin in a pan, cover with water and cook until soft. Drain well.
- Combine all filling ingredients and mix together well.
- Combine oil and water. Lay 3 sheets of filo pastry on a clean, dry bench. Brush a little combined oil and water over them and fold in half. Place some filling at one end, fold edges over and roll up. Brush over a little more combined oil and water and place on baking tray. Repeat with remaining pastry and filling to make 8 spring rolls.
- Bake for 30–40 minutes or until crisp and brown on all sides. Turn during cooking to crisp and brown evenly.

Serve immediately with Sweet Chilli Dipping Sauce (see page 154) and a green salad (see pages 150–1). Also serve with freshly squeezed orange juice.

Sweet Potato and Lentil Burgers with Curry Yoghurt Dressing

Serves 4-6

Just make these once – and you'll want to make them again and again!

½ cup brown lentils
2–3 cups water
1 carrot
500 g sweet potato peeled
1 onion, finely diced
2 teaspoons low-salt soy sauce
1 tablespoon tahini
2 tablespoons finely chopped fresh coriander or chives or parsley
freshly ground black pepper
1 cup wheatgerm

CURRY YOGHURT DRESSING
1 cup low-fat yoghurt
1 teaspoon curry powder
1 teaspoon cumin
1 tablespoon finely grated orange rind

- Wash lentils thoroughly, cover with water and bring to the boil. Remove any foam that rises to the top and simmer for 25–30 minutes or until soft. Drain well.
- Boil carrot and sweet potato until soft. Drain well and mash. Add onion, soy sauce, tahini, herbs and pepper. Shape into round burgers and roll in wheatgerm.
- Place burgers on a tray and refrigerate for 2 hours.
- To make the dressing, combine all ingredients in a blender and blend until smooth.
- Lightly oil a frying pan and heat until hot. Cook burgers on both sides until brown.

Serve with Curry Yoghurt Dressing and a green salad (see pages 150–1).

Serves 4-6

Vegetable Pie

Here are winter vegetables set firm in a creamy sauce, snuggled in a crusty, crunchy pastry case. You can substitute sweet potatoes for the pumpkin for a yummy variation

1 quantity Basic Pastry (see page 157)
1 litre low-fat soymilk or low-fat milk
3/4 cup cornflour
1 teaspoon turmeric
1/8 teaspoon cayenne pepper
2 tablespoons grated parmesan cheese
1 cup chopped spring onion
500 g pumpkin, peeled, cooked, cold
500 g potatoes, peeled, cooked, cold
1/4 cup chopped sun-dried tomatoes, well drained
2 tablespoons sesame seeds

- Preheat oven to 200°C. Roll out pastry to fit a large flan dish.
- Mix enough milk with cornflour to make a paste.
- Place remaining milk, turmeric and cayenne pepper in a saucepan and heat to nearly boiling. Add cornflour mixture and stir until it boils and thickens.
- Stir in parmesan cheese and spring onion and remove from heat.
- Add pumpkin, potato and sun-dried tomato.
- Pour mixture into pastry-lined flan dish. Scatter sesame seeds over.
- Bake for 1 hour or until filling has firmed and pastry is brown.

Serve with a green salad (see pages 150–1).

BASIC RECIPES

ALMOND MILK

Almond milk is a delicious alternative to cow's milk. Almonds provide an easily assimilated source of calcium, a moderate amount of protein and some dietary fibre and contain essential unsaturated fatty acids. Makes 1 cup.

20–30 almonds
boiling water
1 cup water, chilled
vanilla essence to taste (optional)

Place almonds in a small bowl and pour enough boiling water over to cover. Leave to stand for a few minutes. Pour off water, rub off almond skins and process nuts until very fine. Slowly add cold water and process until you have a rich, creamy milk. Add vanilla to taste. Keep refrigerated.

CHARGRILLING

Chargrilling generally refers to a cooking technique where food is placed on a hot pan that has specially designed raised ridges. The ridges give the cooked food a distinctive blackened, lined pattern and a wood-fired, almost smoky flavour. If the pan is very hot before placing food in it, there should be no need to add any oil.

Chargrilled Capsicum

Here are three different methods for roasting a capsicum.

1. Cut capsicum in half and remove seeds. Place under a griller until skin blackens and begins to lift away from flesh. Place in a sealed plastic bag or wrap securely in foil and allow to go completely cold. Peel away blackened skin before using.

2. Insert a long skewer into capsicum. Hold over a hot flame, turning continuously, until skin blackens and bubbles. Place in a sealed plastic bag or wrap securely in foil and allow to go completely cold. Peel away blackened skin before using.

3. Poach capsicum until soft and place immediately in cold water. Drain well. Cut in half. Remove seeds and peel. Chargrill on a lightly oiled, hot chargrill pan. Place in a sealed plastic bag or wrap securely in foil and allow to go completely cold. Peel away blackened skin before using.

Chargrilled Carrots

Cut raw or partly cooked carrots into thin lengths. Preheat a non-stick chargrill pan. Place carrot in pan and chargrill on both sides. If the pan you are using is not non-stick, you will need to lightly oil the surface or lightly oil the carrots before cooking.

Chargrilled Eggplants

Here are three ways to achieve a chargrilled effect with eggplants. In all three, you need to cut eggplant into thin or thick rounds and degorge if necessary (see page 26).

1. Preheat a chargrill pan. Brush a little olive oil on both sides of eggplant slices. Chargrill on both sides.

2. Preheat griller to hot. Brush a little olive oil on both sides of eggplant slices. Grill until both sides are well browned.

3. Brush a little olive oil on both sides of eggplant slices. Lay on a non-stick baking tray and bake in a hot oven for approximately 15–20 minutes or until both sides are well browned.

Chargrilled Mushrooms

Remove mushroom stems. Place skin side down on a hot chargrill pan. Cover and cook for 3–5 minutes. Turn and continue to chargrill until mushrooms are quite soft and well browned.

Chargrilled Pumpkin or Sweet Potato

Cut pumpkin or sweet potato into thin pieces. Preheat a chargrill pan. Brush a little olive oil on both sides of vegetable pieces. Chargrill on both sides until browned and soft, but not so soft that pieces break.

Chargrilled Zucchini

Cook as for carrots.

COUS COUS

1 cup cous cous
1 cup boiling water

Place cous cous in a bowl. Pour over boiling water and cover with plastic wrap. Stand for 5 minutes. Remove cover and lightly fluff with a fork. For extra flavour add some finely chopped fresh mint or finely grated lemon or orange rind. Serves 4.

CUSTARD (low-fat)

INGREDIENT	MAKES 2 CUPS	MAKES 3 CUPS	MAKES 1 LITRE	MAKES 2 LITRES
MILK	2 cups	3 cups	1 litre	2 litres
CORNFLOUR	½ cup	¾ cup	1 cup	2 cups
VANILLA ESSENCE	1 teaspoon	1½ teaspoons	2 teaspoons	1 tablespoon
ORANGE ZEST	2 teaspoons	1 tablespoon	1½ tablespoons	2 tablespoons
APPLE JUICE CONCENTRATE	¼ cup	⅓ cup	½ cup	1 cup
LOW-FAT YOGHURT	½ cup	¾ cup	1 cup	2 cups

Mix a little milk with cornflour to make a paste. Add cornflour mixture to remaining milk, vanilla essence and orange zest in a saucepan. Slowly bring to the boil, stirring continuously until custard begins to thicken. Remove custard from the heat and stir in apple juice concentrate and yoghurt. Serve hot or cold. Cold custard will set firm.

DRESSINGS

Balsamic Vinaigrette

4 tablespoons balsamic vinegar
½–1 teaspoon crushed garlic
2 tablespoons safflower or olive oil

Combine all ingredients in a screwtop jar and shake well. Keep sealed and refrigerated. Makes ⅓ cup.

Chinese Dressing

½ cup freshly squeezed orange juice
¾ cup mirin
2 teaspoons fish sauce
1 teaspoon Chinese five-spice powder
1 tablespoon apple juice concentrate
1 cm piece fresh ginger, peeled finely chopped
2 tablespoons finely chopped spring onions

Combine all ingredients in a screwtop jar and shake well. Keep sealed and refrigerated. Makes ¾ cup.

Creamy Mayonnaise

200 g low-fat yoghurt
1 tablespoon low-fat cholesterol-free mayonnaise (see page 22)
1 tablespoon apple juice concentrate
1 teaspoon dry mustard
¼ teaspoon freshly ground black pepper

Combine all ingredients in a small bowl and whisk well. Keep sealed and refrigerated in an airtight jar. Makes ½ cup.

French Dressing

⅔ cup white wine vinegar
⅓ cup freshly squeezed lemon juice
4 tablespoons apple juice concentrate
pinch of salt
pinch of freshly ground black pepper

Combine all ingredients in a screwtop jar and shake well. Keep sealed and refrigerated. Makes 1½ cups.

Honey, Soy and Sesame Dressing

2 tablespoons white wine vinegar
2 tablespoons low-salt soy sauce
2 tablespoons honey, warmed
1 tablespoon water
2 tablespoons sesame oil

Place all ingredients except oil in a screwtop jar and shake well. Slowly whisk in oil. Keep sealed and refrigerated. Makes ½ cup.

Red Pepper Mayo

1 red capsicum, halved and seeded
1 tablespoon low-fat, cholesterol-free mayonnaise (see page 22)
2 teaspoons sweet chilli sauce (see page 19)
200 ml plain low-fat yoghurt
freshly ground black pepper
1 tablespoon finely chopped chives

Blanch capsicum in boiling water. Cool and chop roughly. Place with remaining ingredients, except chives, in a food processor and blend until smooth. Add chives. Store in a jar in the refrigerator and shake well before using. Makes ¾ cup.

Spicy Oriental Dressing

2 tablespoons freshly squeezed lime or lemon juice
1 teaspoon finely chopped, seeded, fresh red chilli or sweet chilli sauce (see page 19)
3 tablespoons low-salt soy sauce
2 tablespoons apple juice concentrate
1 tablespoon fish sauce (see page 18)
1 clove garlic, crushed
1 cm-piece fresh ginger, peeled, finely chopped or 1 teaspoon finely chopped pickled ginger (see page 21)

Combine all ingredients in a screwtop jar and shake well. Keep sealed and refrigerated. Makes ½ cup.

Tangy Tahini Dressing

1 tablespoon honey, warmed
200 g low-fat yoghurt
2 tablespoons hulled tahini paste (see page 23)
1–2 tablespoons freshly squeezed lemon juice
½–1 teaspoon crushed garlic

Combine all ingredients in a screwtop jar and shake well. Keep sealed and refrigerated. Makes ⅔ cup.

GREEN SALAD

Vegetarian diets need plenty of vitamin C to assist the absorption of iron in the diet. Complementing vegetarian main meals with a green salad is just one way to do this. There is literally no end to the variety of greens available to make the classic 'green salad' that complements and enhances the nutritional value of a vegetarian meal. They all have wonderful flavours and complement each other with a mixture of delicate, assertive, buttery, mustardy, peppery, tart, lemony and nutty tastes. They come in all shades of green and reddish-purple colours with feathery, curly, crinkly, soft or frilled foliage, which look good in the salad bowl.

It is important to wash the leaves in lots of cold water to remove sand and grit that tends to get caught in the foliage grooves. Be gentle though, as the leaves bruise easily. Dry the washed leaves in a salad spinner or in between paper towelling or wrap loosely in a tea towel.

If you follow these guidelines you will find that a good combination of the freshest greens hardly needs to be dressed. Simply add handfuls of lovely, fresh, micronutrient-rich herbs like chives, basil, coriander, parsley, mint, oregano or thyme. Grated lemon or orange rind, seeds such as poppy or sesame seeds, and chopped nuts add even more nutrient value and plenty of extra flavour. For extra vitamin C in your green salad, add lots of thinly sliced red and green capsicum. There are no rules for the quantity of greens to allow per person, but about 50 g is a good guide.

If you do dress the salad (see pages 147–150), use the absolute minimum and toss through just before serving. If you are using an oil-based dressing, make sure it's a good-quality virgin oil. The leaves should be dry so the oil coats the leaves and imparts a delicious, fruity oil flavour.

Keep your eye out for names such as radicchio, red butter, green and red oakleaf, romaine, red perella, baby bok choy, spinach, collard, red and green mustard, sorrel, red and green chard, Belgian endive, curly endive, chicory, cress, watercress, red-beet greens, kale and frisée. They are all loaded with nutrients such as vitamins A and C and are high in iron, calcium and potassium. Best of all, they are a very low-kilojoule food.

GRILLED TOMATOES

Cut tomatoes in half. Place on a paper-lined non-stick baking tray. Place under a griller to warm and brown. For added flavour, sprinkle tomatoes with a little rock salt, freshly ground black pepper, basil, oregano or a little olive oil that has been flavoured with crushed garlic.

PASTRY (basic)

This recipe makes enough pastry to fit the base of a large pie dish or the bottom and top of a small pie dish.

2 cups unbleached wholemeal plain flour
½ cup unbleached white plain flour
2 tablespoons olive oil
2 tablespoons lemon juice
½–¾ cup chilled mineral water

Combine first 4 ingredients in a food processor and blend until mixture resembles fine breadcrumbs. Keep motor running and add enough mineral water to make a soft, pliable dough. Alternatively, combine first 4 ingredients in a bowl and work quickly with your fingertips until mixture resembles fine breadcrumbs. Add a little mineral water at a time while you work the dough to a soft, pliable consistency.

Wrap pastry in plastic wrap and refrigerate for 30 minutes. Lightly oil a pie dish. Flour a clean, dry bench and, using a wooden rolling pin, roll pastry out to fit pie dish. Transfer pastry to pie dish. Press firmly into base and sides and the edges. Prick with a fork and add filling.

PESTO

Parmesan cheese gives pesto its typical flavour, but you can leave the cheese out and still have a delicious pesto that can be used to flavour all sorts of dishes. Makes ¼ cup.

50 g fresh basil leaves, stems removed
¼ cup pine nuts
1–2 teaspoons crushed garlic
1 tablespoon olive oil
1 tablespoon grated parmesan cheese (optional)
pinch of salt
pinch of freshly ground black pepper

- Combine basil, pine nuts and garlic in a food processor and process until smooth.
- While food processor is still operating, drizzle in the oil and cheese.
- Add salt and pepper.

RED PESTO

This pesto makes a delicious change to the traditional green pesto. Makes ½ cup.

1–2 chargrilled red capsicums (see pages 144–5)
100 g fresh basil leaves, stems removed
½ cup pine nuts
1–2 teaspoons crushed garlic
1 tablespoon olive oil
1–2 tablespoons grated parmesan cheese (optional)
pinch of salt
pinch of freshly ground black pepper

- Combine capsicums, basil, pine nuts and garlic in a food processor and process until smooth.
- While food processor is still operating, drizzle in oil and cheese.
- Add salt and pepper.

NUT BUTTERS

These yummy butters will give you a taste of the good oil (unsaturated fat). They are ideal as a sandwich spread or a topping for baked potatoes or baked sweet potatoes. Add as garnish to an Asian-style salad or Sunday roast vegetables for a fabulous taste.

Cashew and Sesame Butter

3 tablespoons dry roasted, salt-free cashews
1 tablespoon sesame seeds
1 tablespoon safflower oil

In a food processor, process all ingredients to a paste consistency. Cover and refrigerate.

Mixed Nuts and Seeds Butter

1 tablespoon dry roasted salt-free peanuts or brazil nuts
2 tablespoons dry roasted, salt-free cashews
2 tablespoons sunflower seeds
2 tablespoons pumpkin seeds
1 tablespoon sesame seeds

In a food processor, process all ingredients to a paste consistency. Cover and refrigerate.

SAUCES

Apricot Sauce

1 cup sugar-free apricot jam
1 cup water
1 tablespoon Amaretto liqueur
1 teaspoon grated orange zest

Place all ingredients in a saucepan and stir continuously until jam breaks down and begins to thicken. The longer you cook the sauce, the richer the flavour and the thicker the consistency. Makes 2 cups.

Orange Citrus Sauce

2 cups freshly squeezed orange juice
2 tablespoons cornflour
grated rind of 1 orange
grated rind of 1 lemon or lime
½ cup apple juice concentrate

Mix a little orange juice and cornflour together to make a paste. Place remaining orange juice, rind and apple juice concentrate in a saucepan. Add cornflour mixture and slowly bring to the boil, stirring continuously until sauce boils and thickens. Makes 2½ cups.

Sweet Chilli Dipping Sauce

2 tablespoons sweet chilli sauce (see page 19)
¼ cup rice wine vinegar (see page 25)
1–2 tablespoons apple juice concentrate

Combine all ingredients in a bowl and mix well. Makes ½ cup.

Tofu Cream

375 g silken tofu (see page 18)
2 teaspoons vanilla essence
1–2 tablespoons apple juice concentrate or honey

Combine all ingredients in a bowl and whip until smooth. Refrigerate until firm. Makes 1½ cups.

WHITE SAUCE (low-fat)

INGREDIENT	MAKES 1 CUP	MAKES 2 CUPS	MAKES 3 CUPS	MAKES 1 LITRE
CORNFLOUR	2 tablespoons	¼ cup	½ cup	1 cup
LOW-FAT MILK	1 cup	2 cups	3 cups	1 litre
BAY LEAVES	2	4	6	8

Mix cornflour with a little milk to make a paste. Pour remaining milk into a saucepan and heat to near boiling. Add cornflour paste and bay leaves and stir continuously until sauce boils and thickens. Remove bay leaves. Add pepper to taste. Use immediately.

TOFU (grilled)

500 g firm tofu (see page 18), well drained

Cut tofu into even pieces and lay on a paper-lined non-stick baking tray. Place under a hot griller and grill on both sides until crisp and browned. Before grilling tofu can be marinated in any of the following:

- low-salt soy sauce and finely chopped fresh ginger
- Spicy Oriental Dressing (see page 149)
- sesame oil, low-salt soy sauce and garlic
- sweet chilli sauce (see page 19)
- freshly squeezed orange juice, finely chopped fresh ginger and sesame seeds
- Sichuan Paste (see page 23)
- Hoi Sin Sauce (see page 18)
- low-salt soy sauce, honey and sesame seeds or finely chopped fresh ginger

VEGETABLE STOCKS

Vecon Stock

Makes 1 cup

1–2 teaspoons stock paste (see page 24)
1 cup boiling water

Dissolve stock paste in boiling water and use as required.

Miso Stock

Makes 1 cup

1 teaspoon–1 tablespoon miso paste (see page 22)
1 cup boiling water

Dissolve miso paste in boiling water and use as required.

Vegetable Stock

Makes 1 litre

2 litres water
4 brown onions, skin on, cut in half
6 celery stalks with green foliage, chopped
4 carrots, chopped
6 bay leaves
1 cup freshly chopped parsley
6–10 peppercorns
pinch of salt

Place all ingredients in a large saucepan and bring to the boil. Simmer for 2 hours or until reduced by half. Strain. Discard vegetables and use stock as required. For a more concentrated stock, discard all vegetables except carrots and onion flesh. Purée these vegetables and stir back into strained liquid.

You could substitute wine, salt-free tomato juice or orange juice for some of the water. You could also add chopped fresh ginger, garlic cloves or – chillies. However, it is best to add ingredients with specific and dominant flavours to the recipe itself, rather than the stock.

INDEX

R